Teacher Essentials
coloring book
Volume 1

by Robbin Briley

Teacher Essentials Coloring Book, Volume 1

Divinelyartistic Creations

Chocowinity, NC 27817

For Dillon and Madison

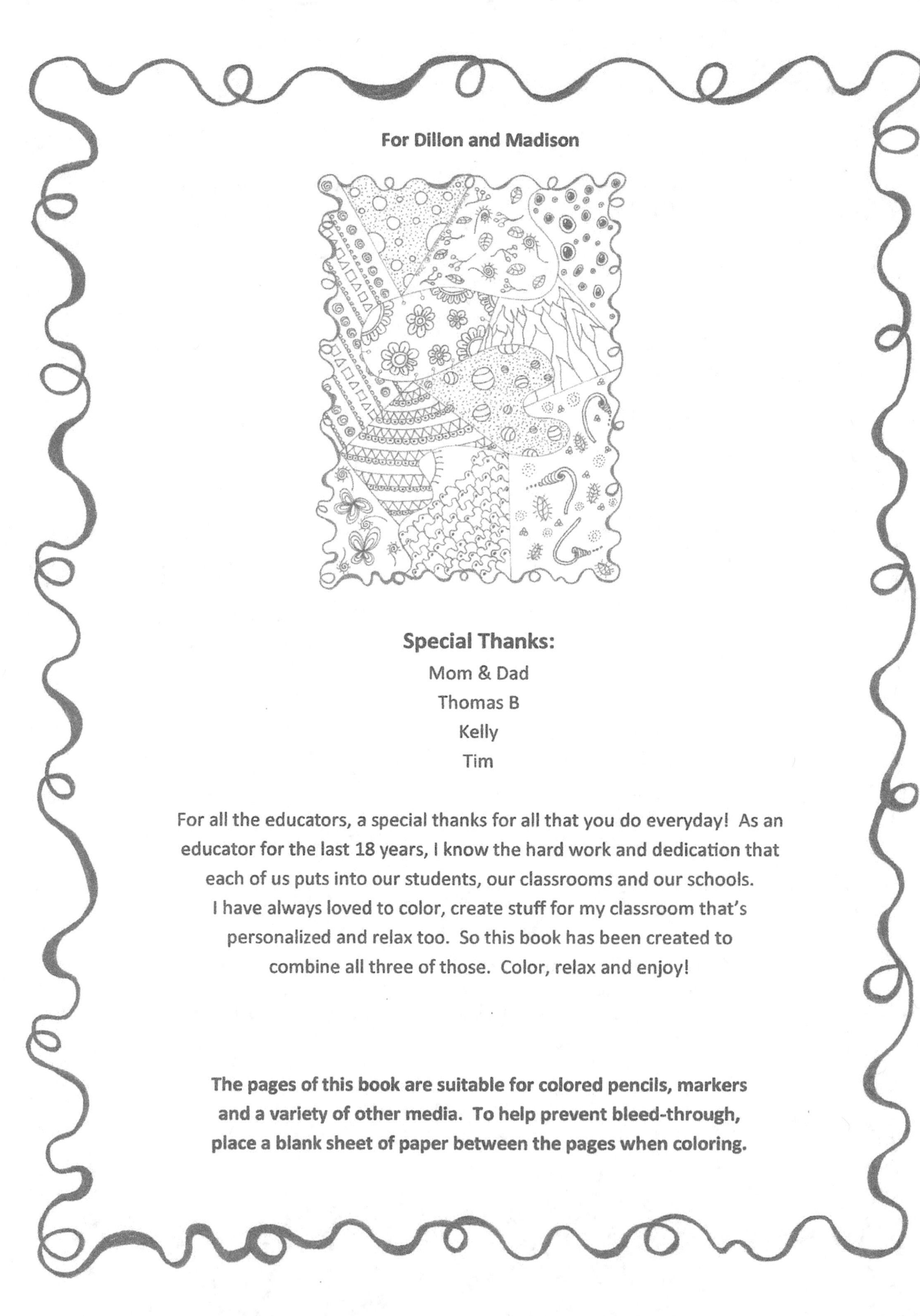

Special Thanks:
Mom & Dad
Thomas B
Kelly
Tim

For all the educators, a special thanks for all that you do everyday! As an
educator for the last 18 years, I know the hard work and dedication that
each of us puts into our students, our classrooms and our schools.
I have always loved to color, create stuff for my classroom that's
personalized and relax too. So this book has been created to
combine all three of those. Color, relax and enjoy!

**The pages of this book are suitable for colored pencils, markers
and a variety of other media. To help prevent bleed-through,
place a blank sheet of paper between the pages when coloring.**

Education is the most powerful weapon which you can use to change the world.

-Nelson Mandela

T errific

E nergetic

A ble

C heerful

H ardworking

E nthusiastic

R emarkable

By Divinelyartistic Creations 2016

By Divinelyartistic Creations ©

By Divinely artistic Creations 2016

By Divinelyartistic Creations © 2016

Gg

© By Divinely Artistic Creations 2016

By Pinnely Artistic Creations 2016

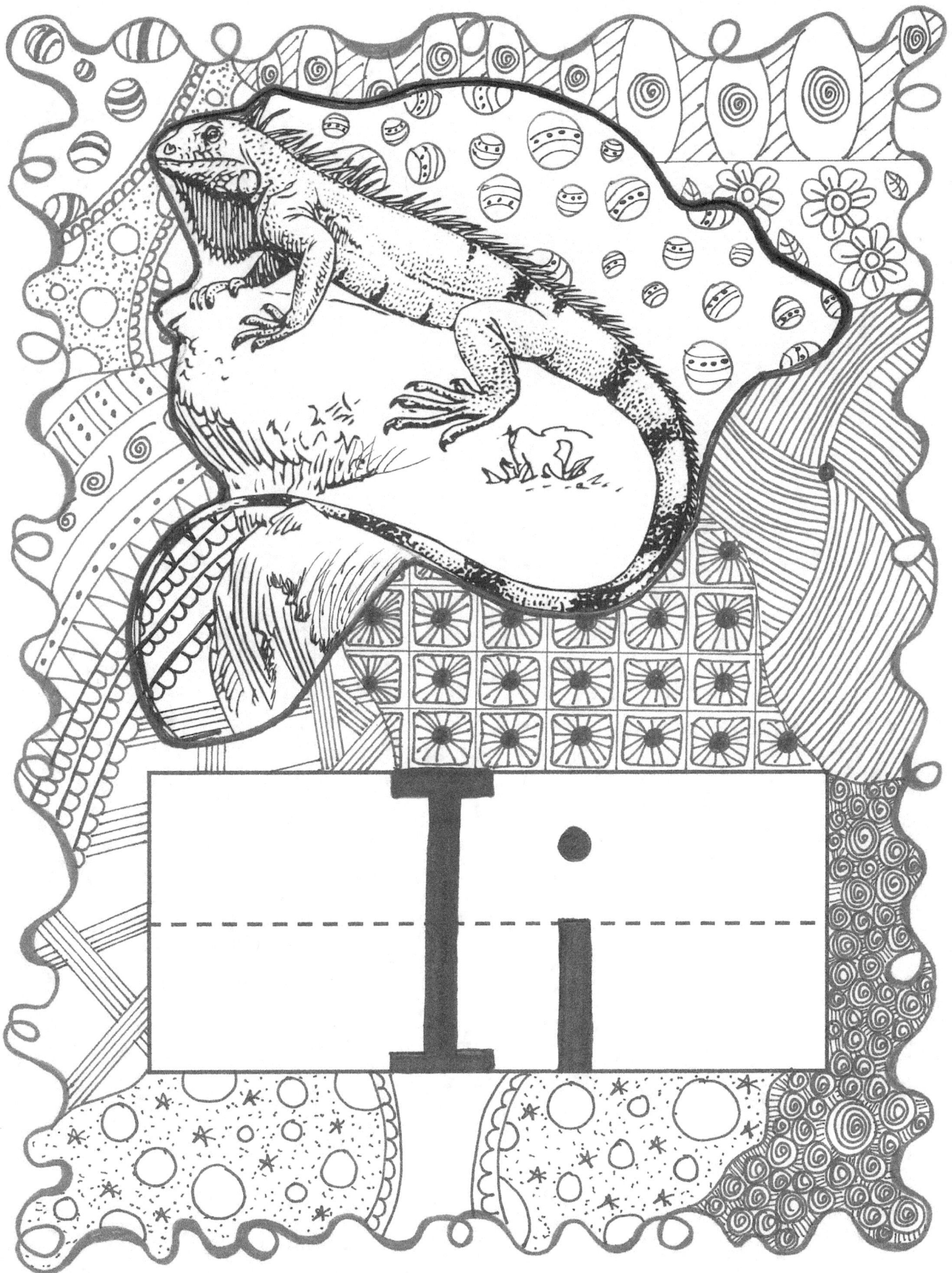

Jj

Divinely artistic Creations 2016©

Divinelyartistic Creations 2016©

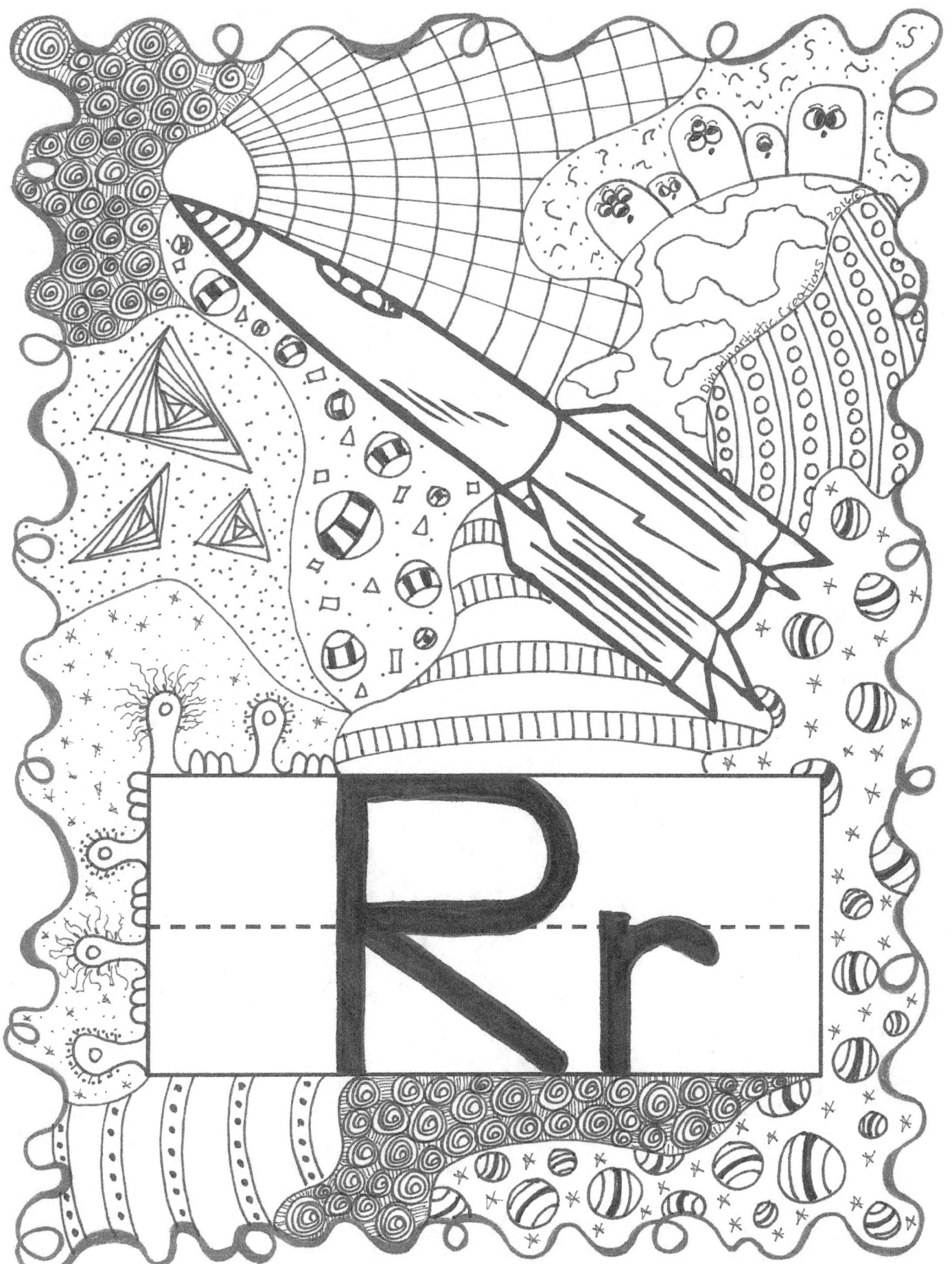

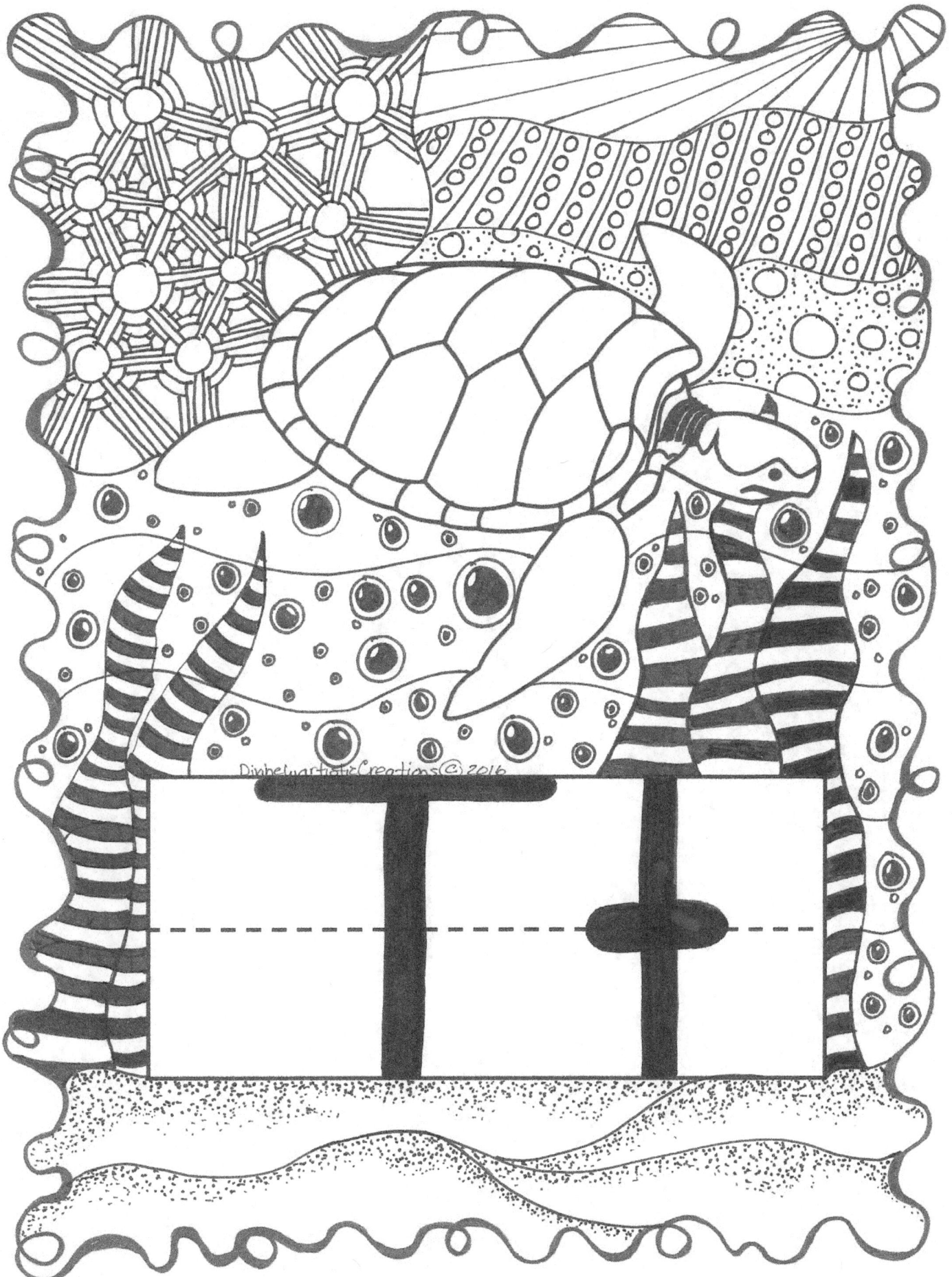

DinhelwartisticCreations© 2016

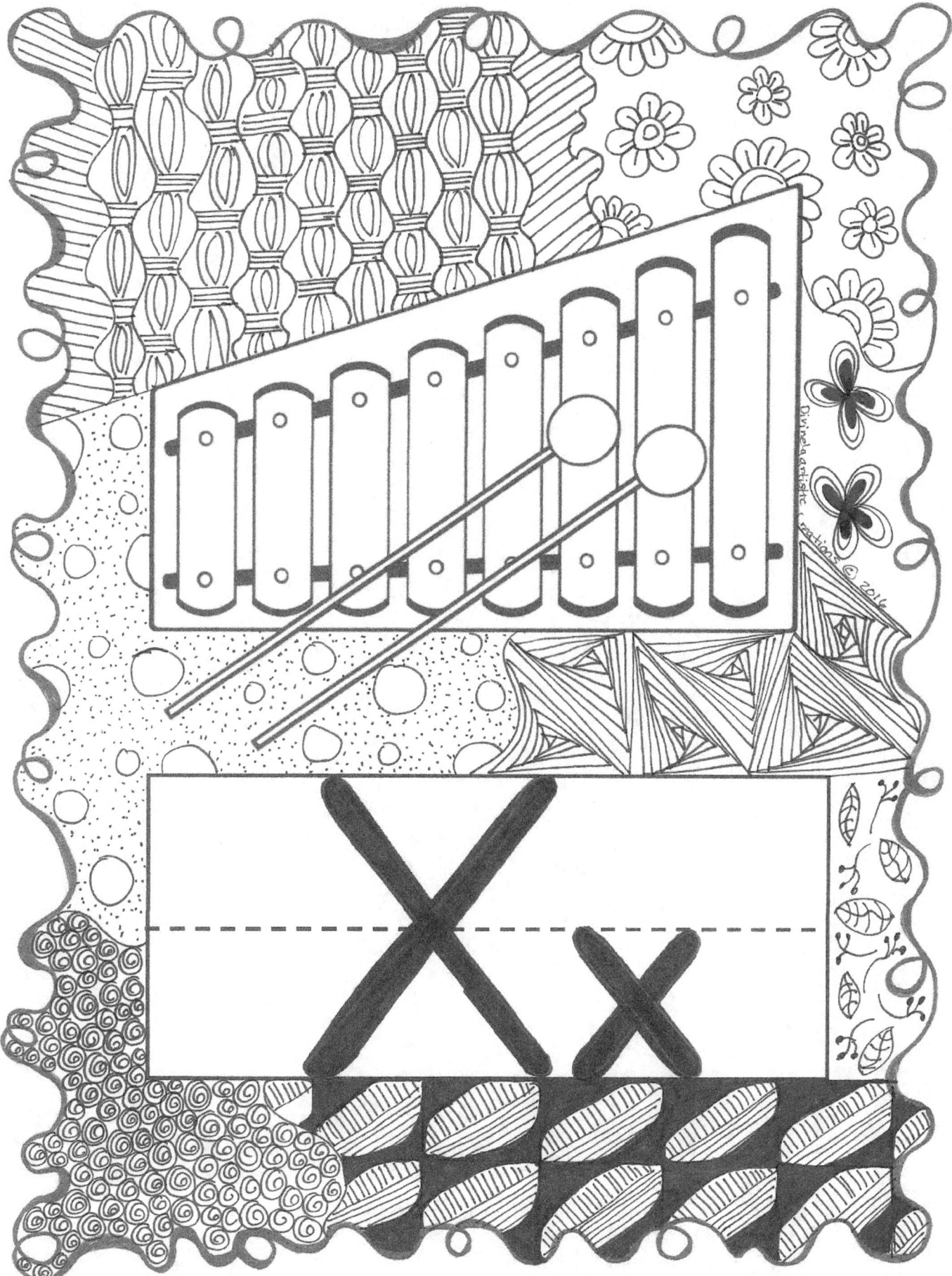

Divinely artistic Creations © 2016

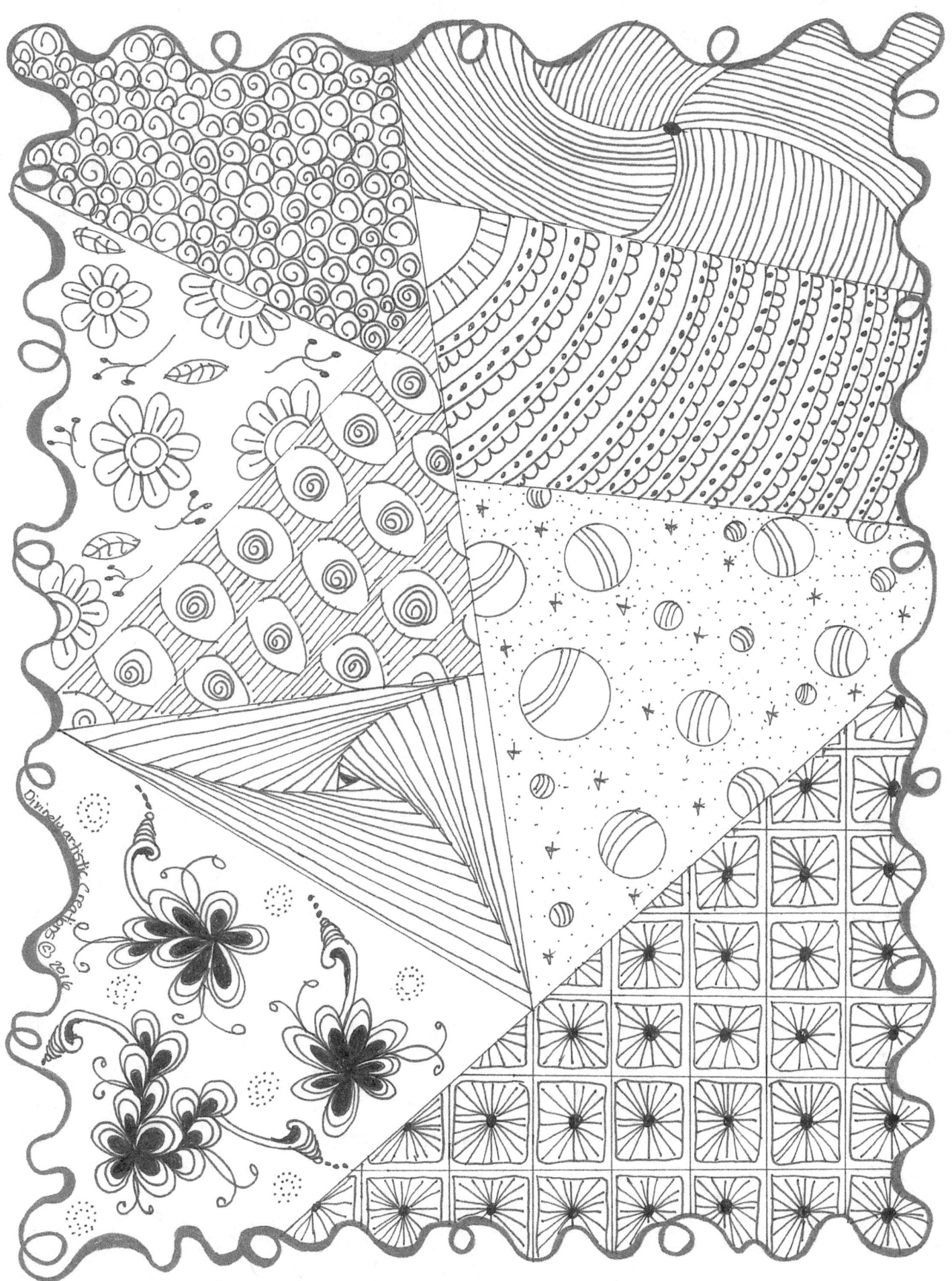

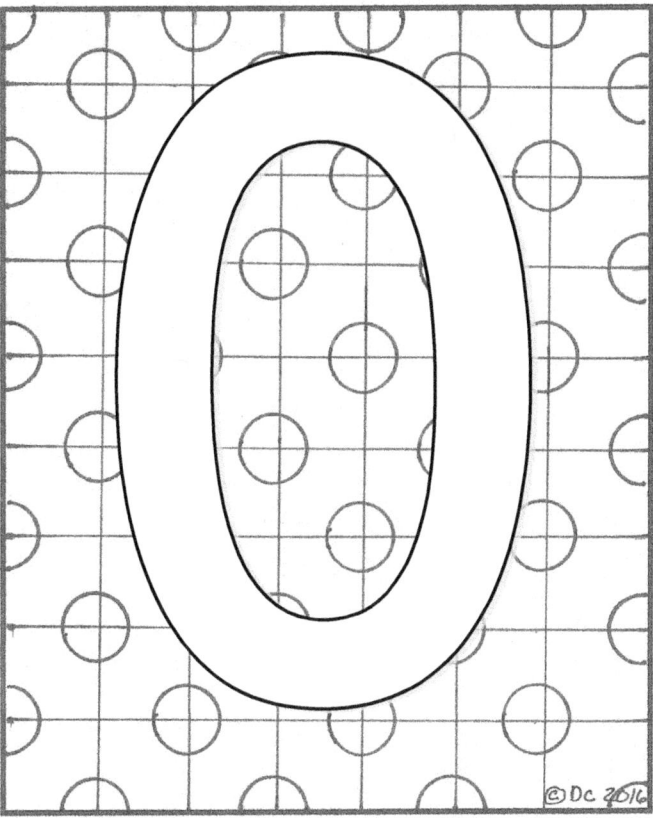

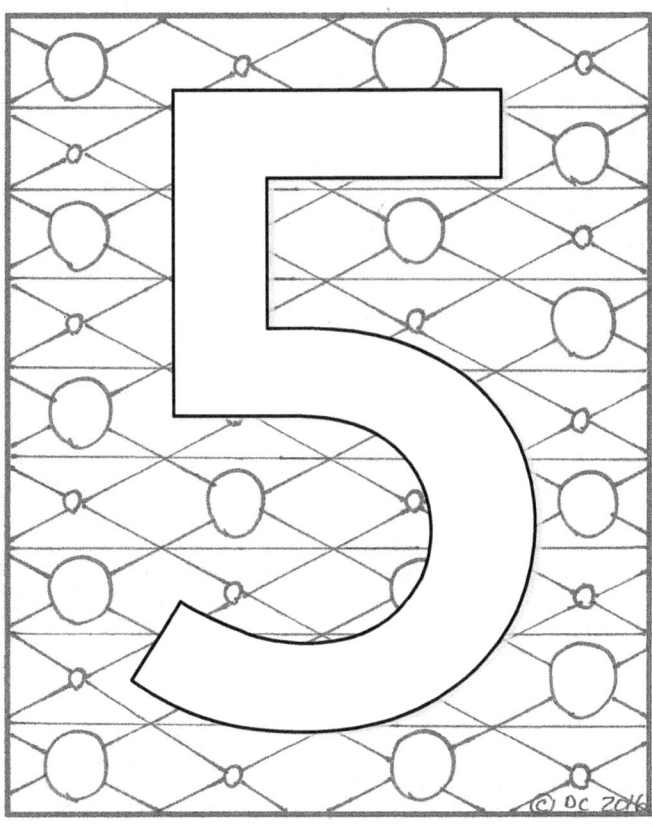

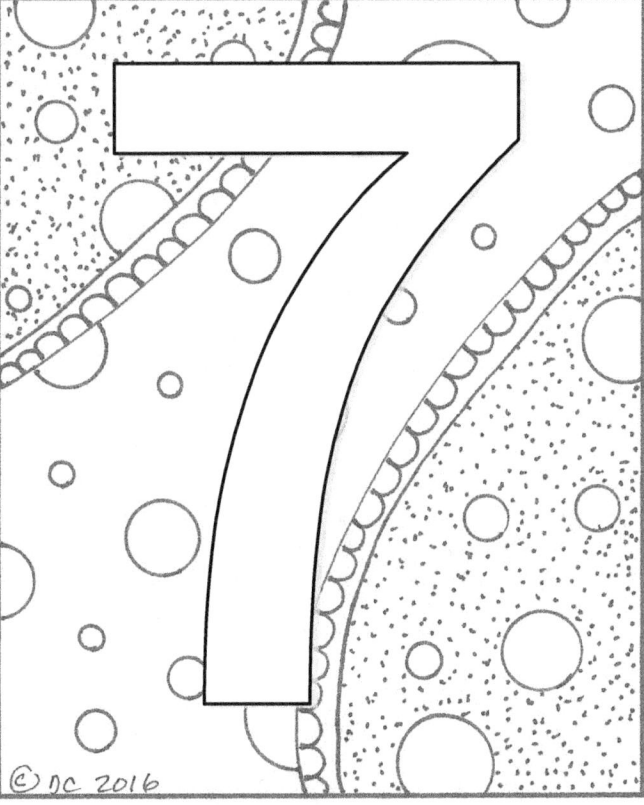

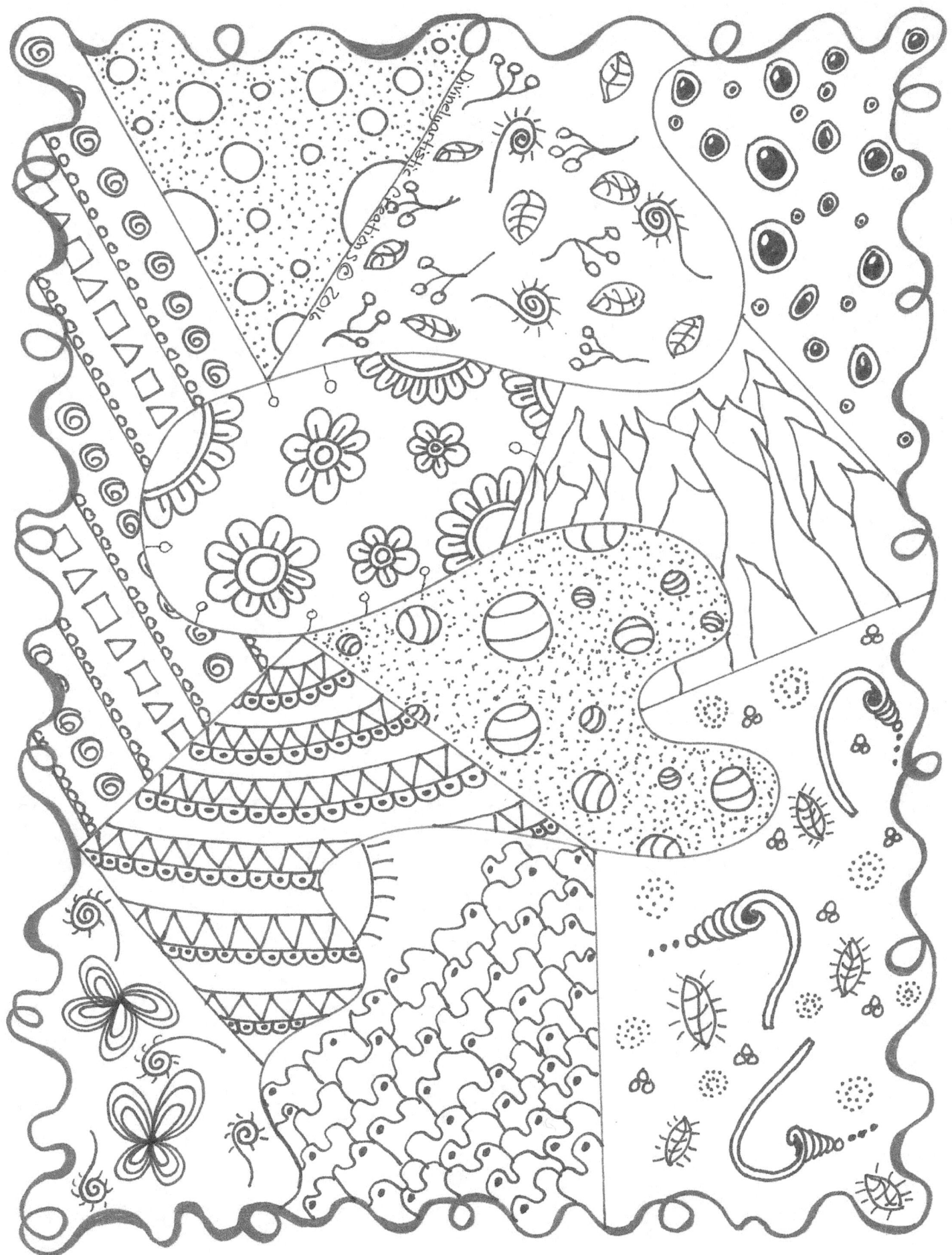

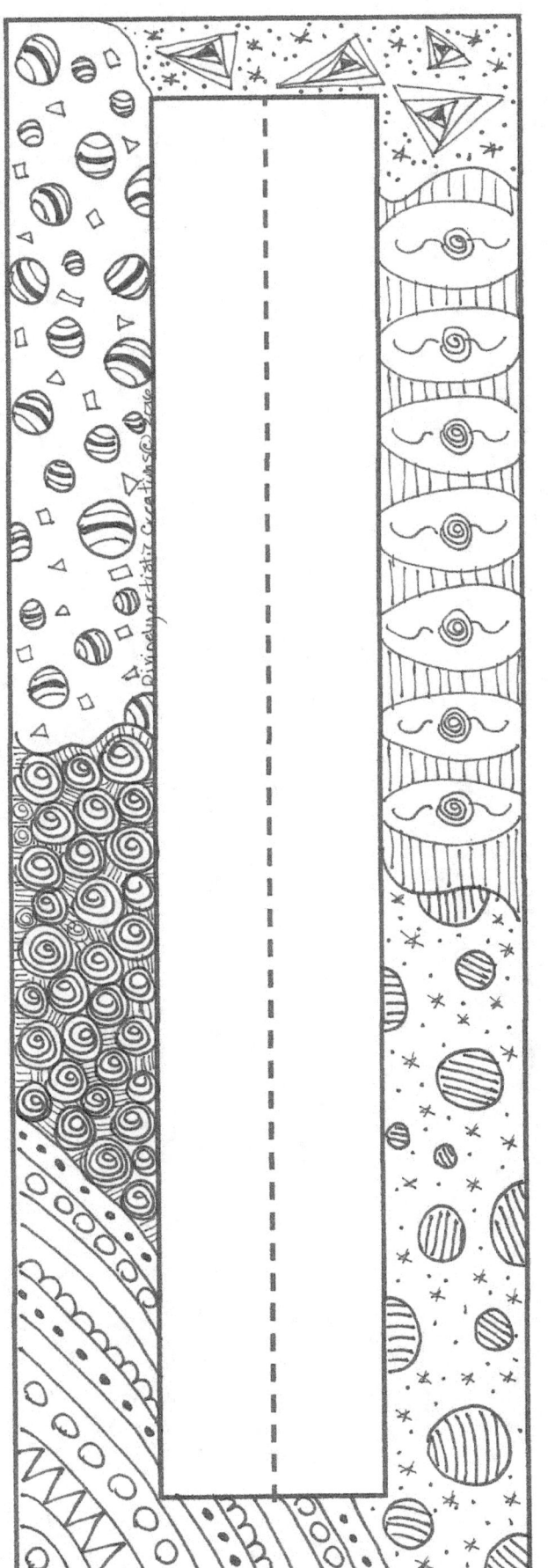

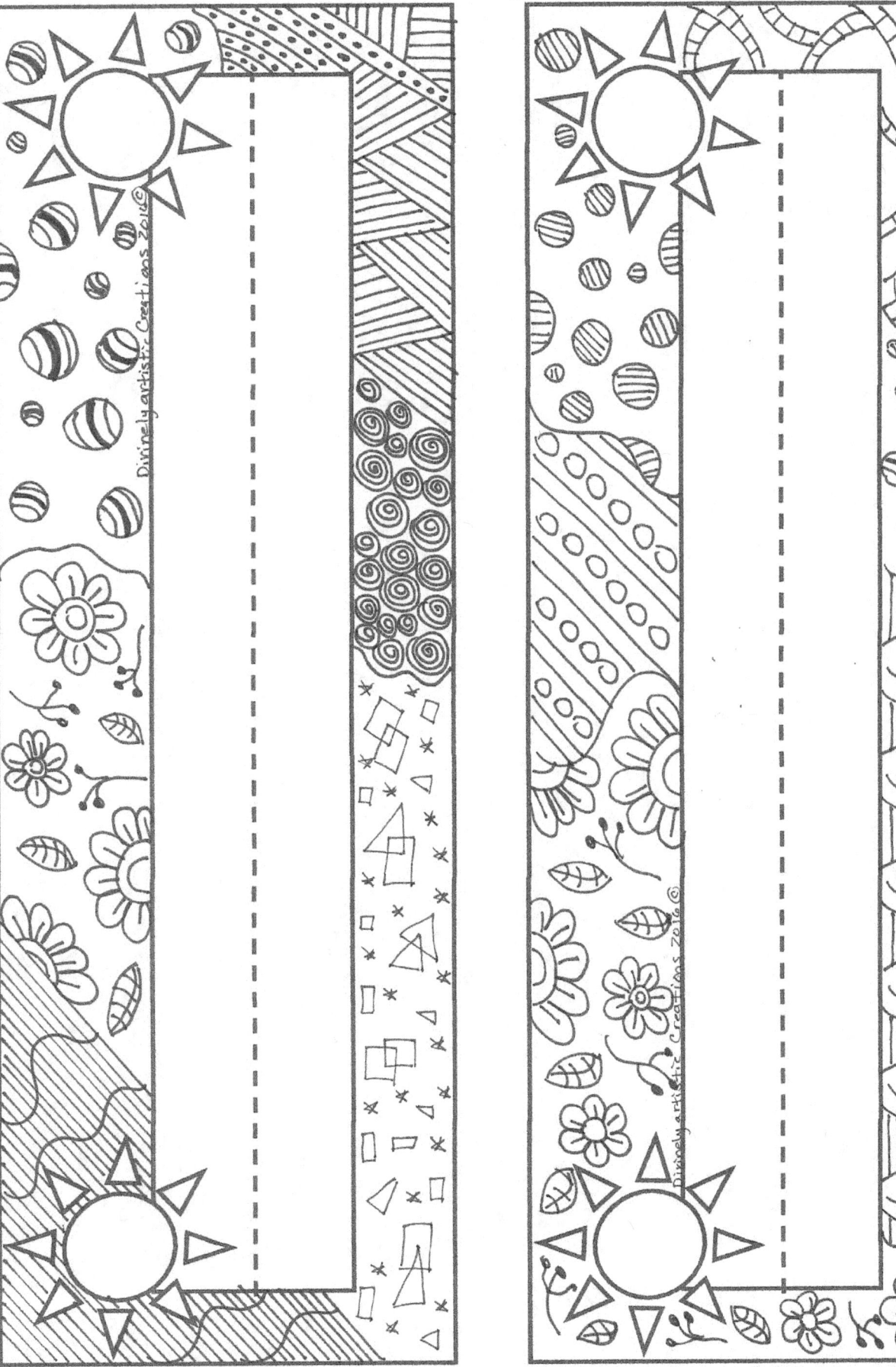

Divinely artistic Creations 2016 ©

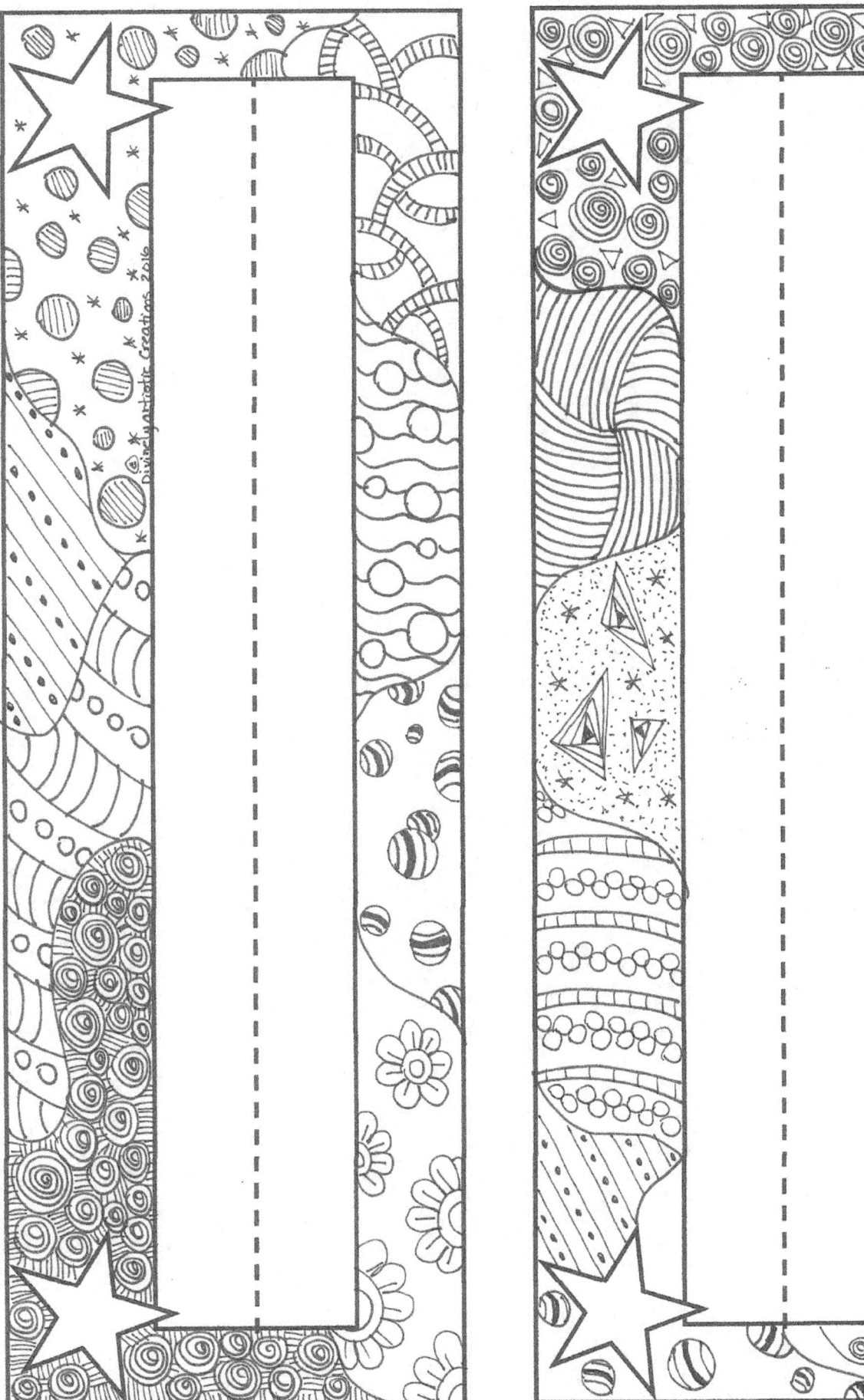

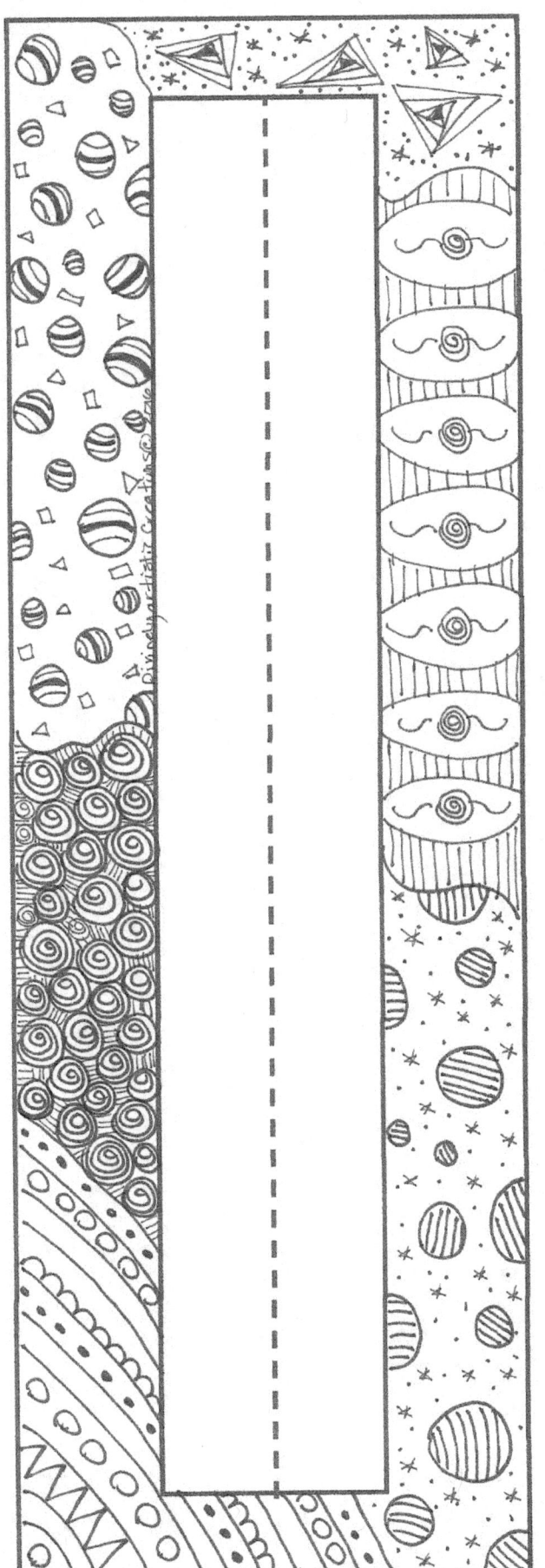

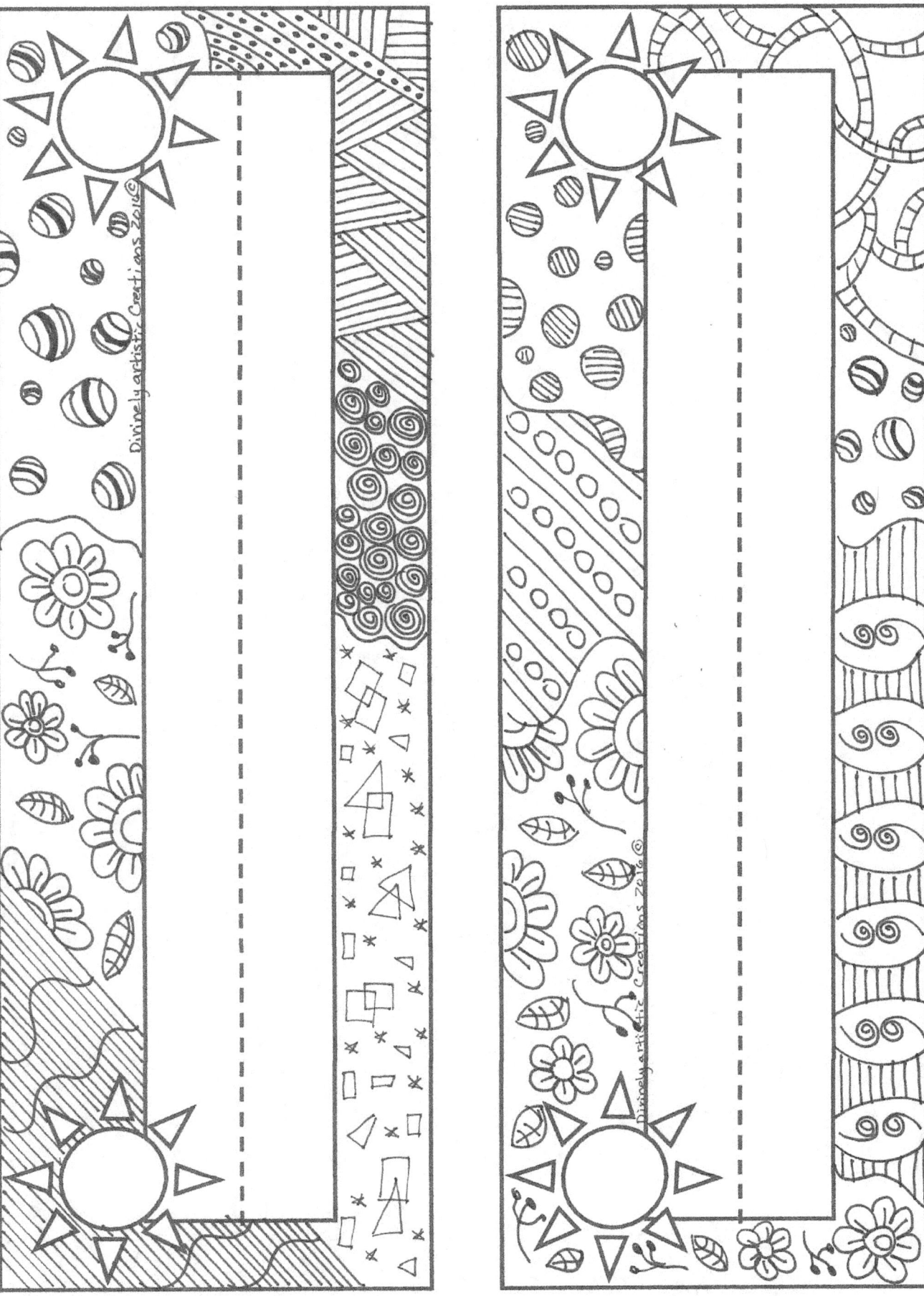

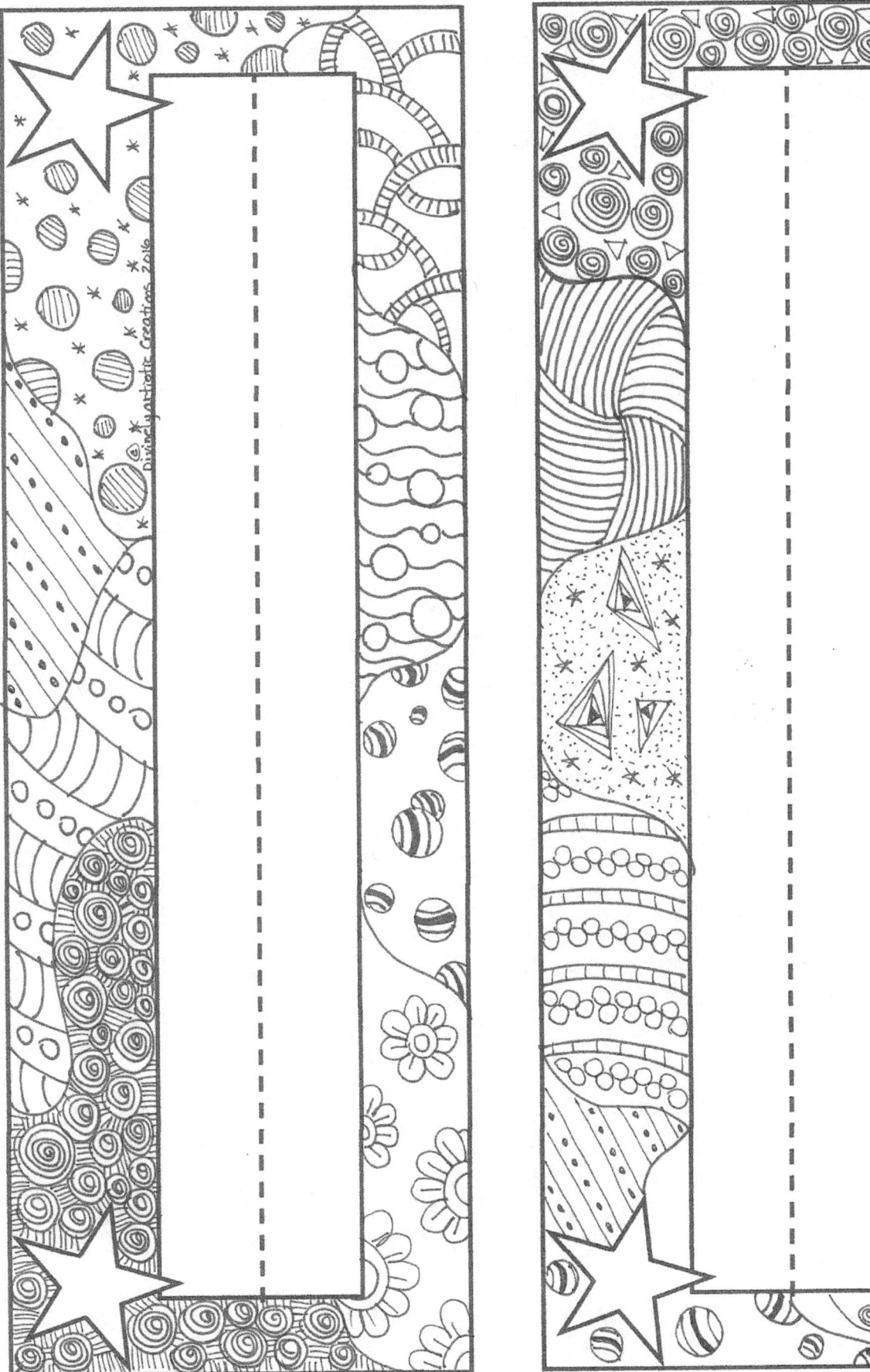

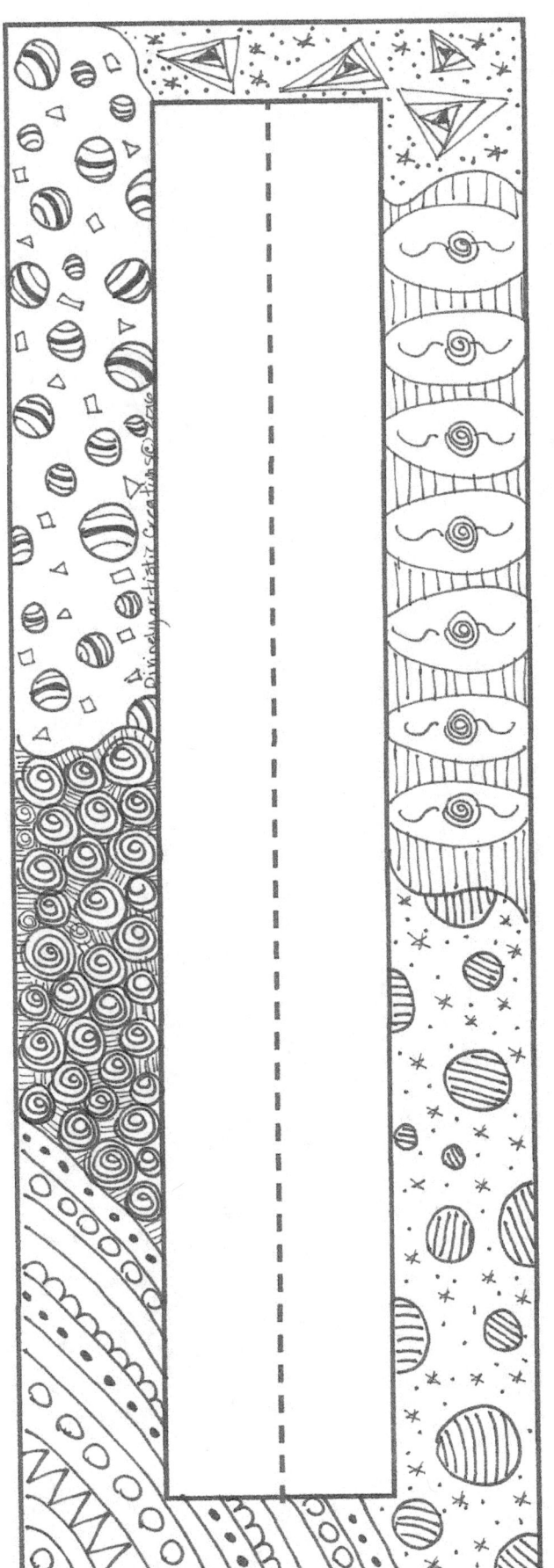

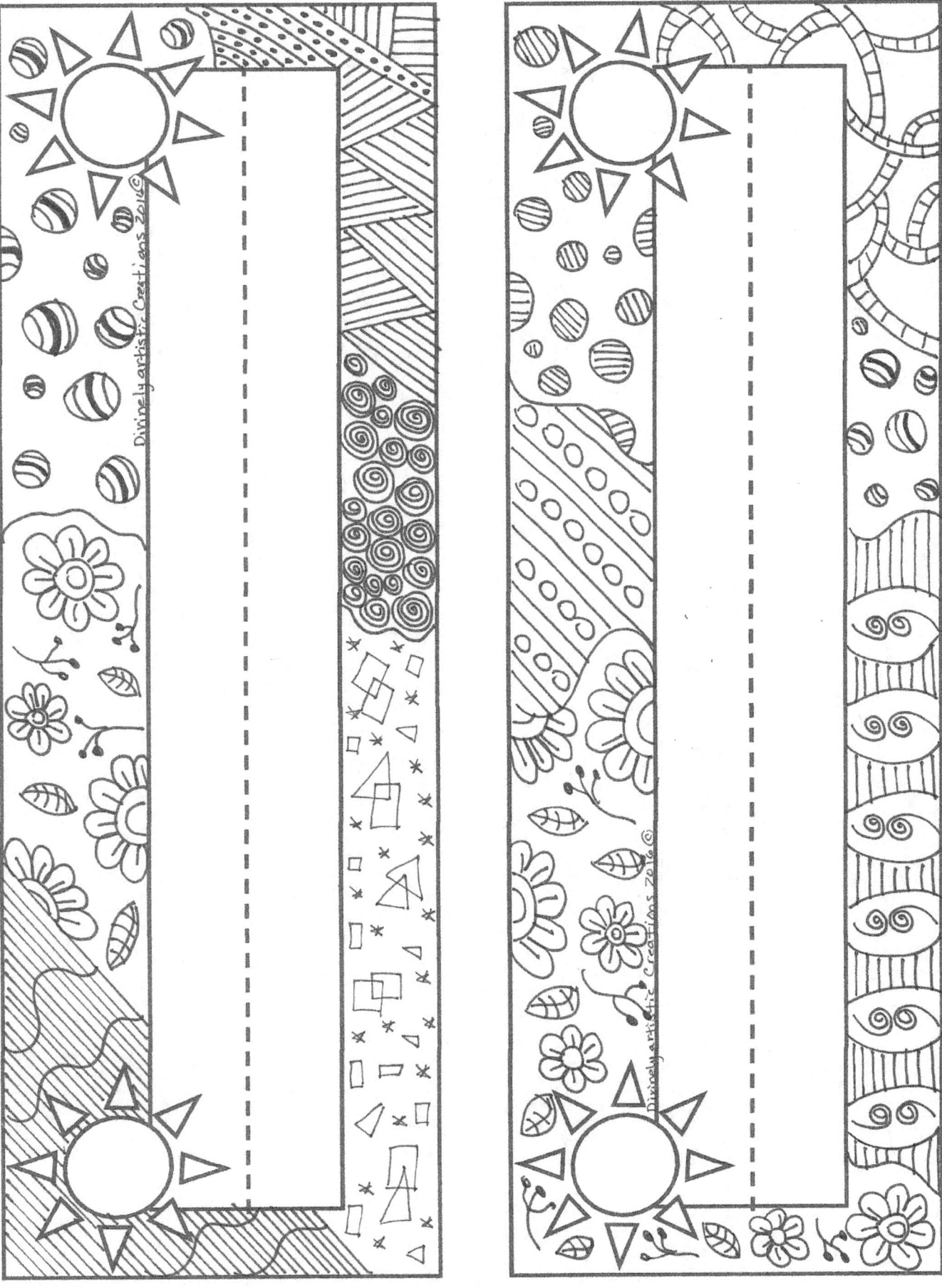

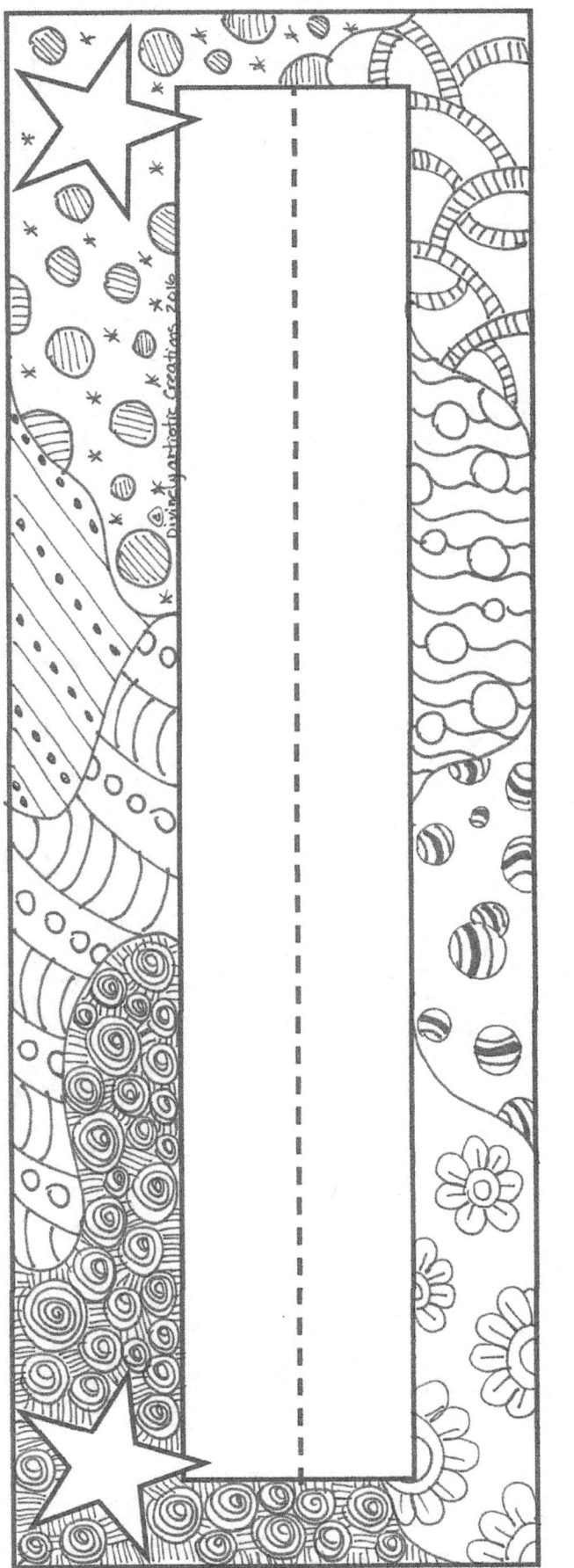
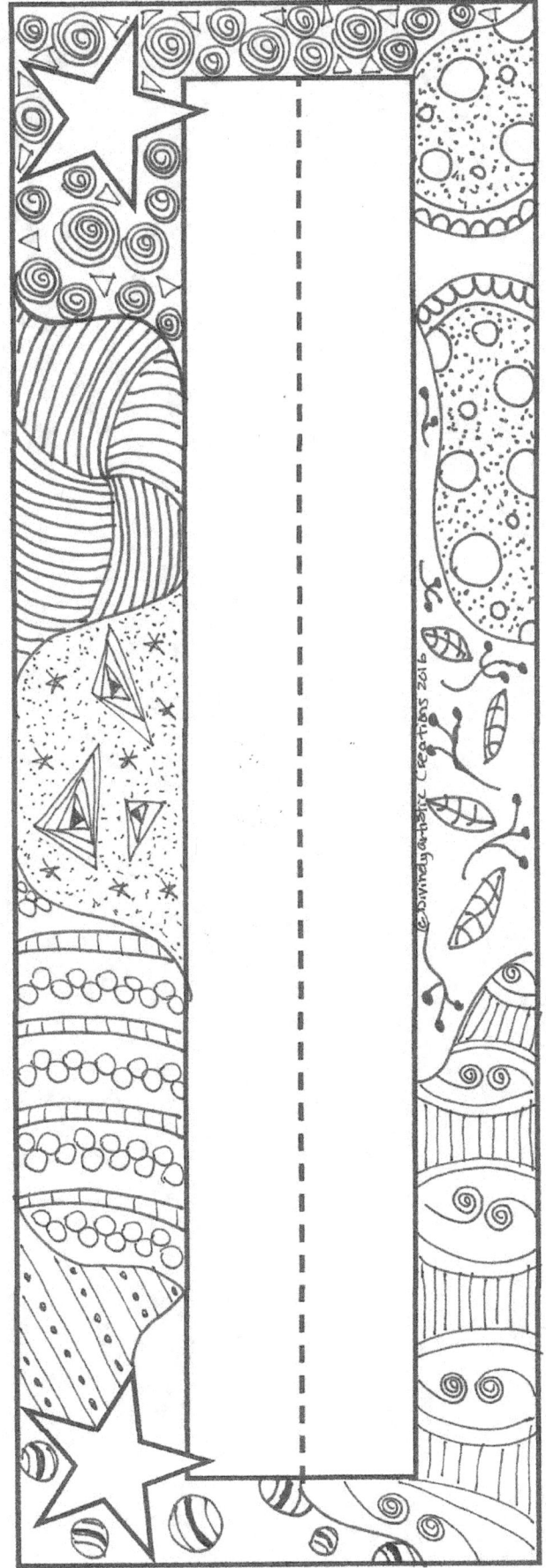

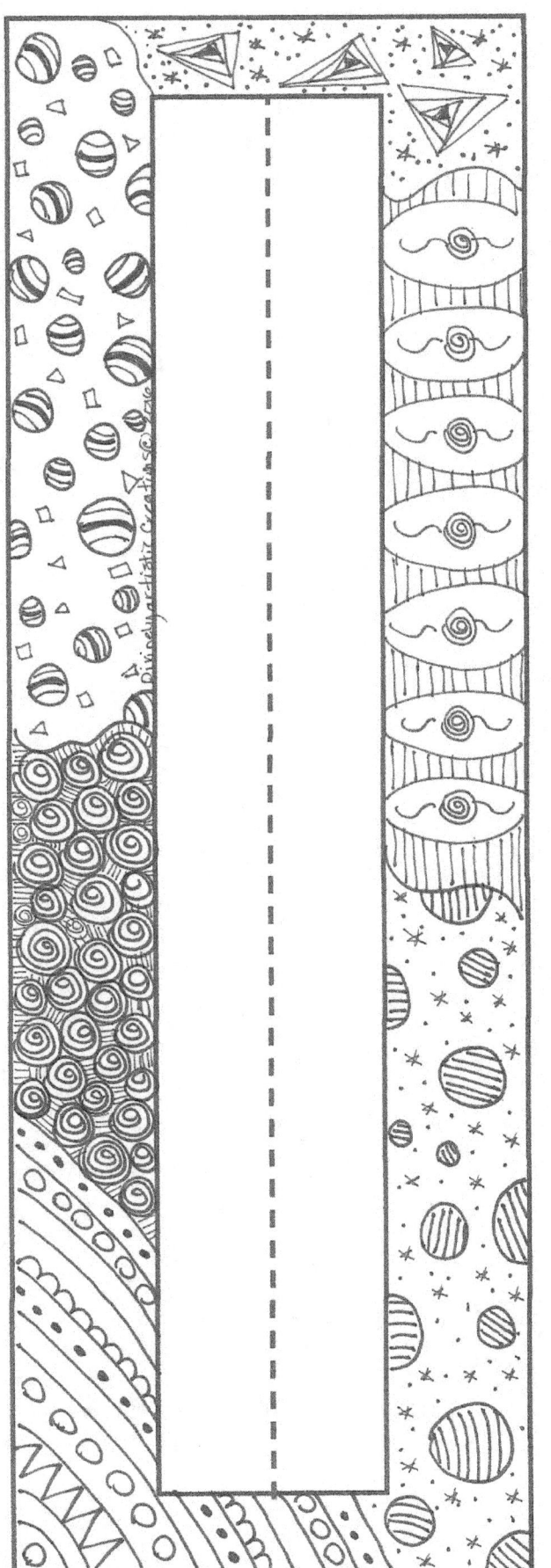

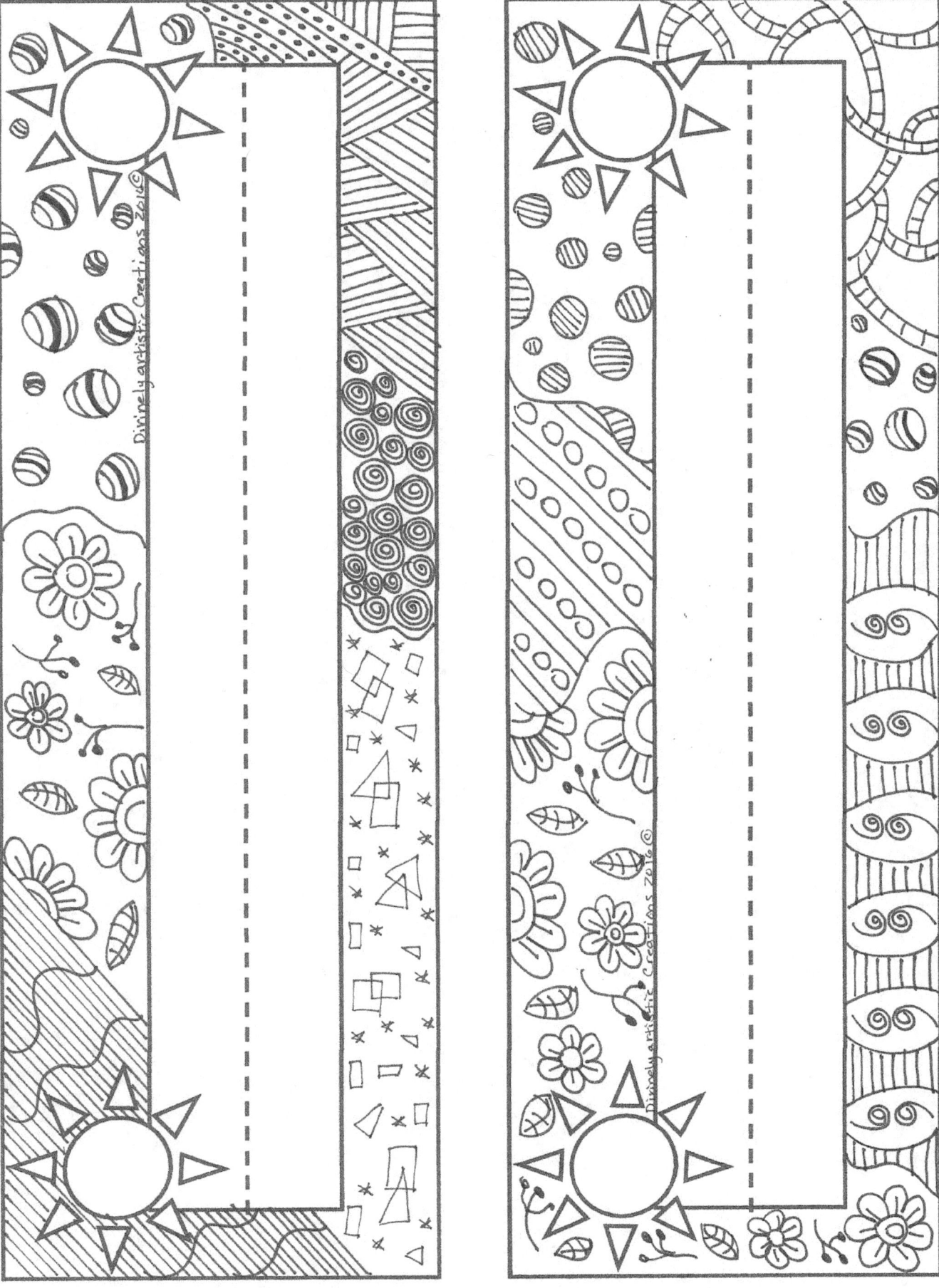

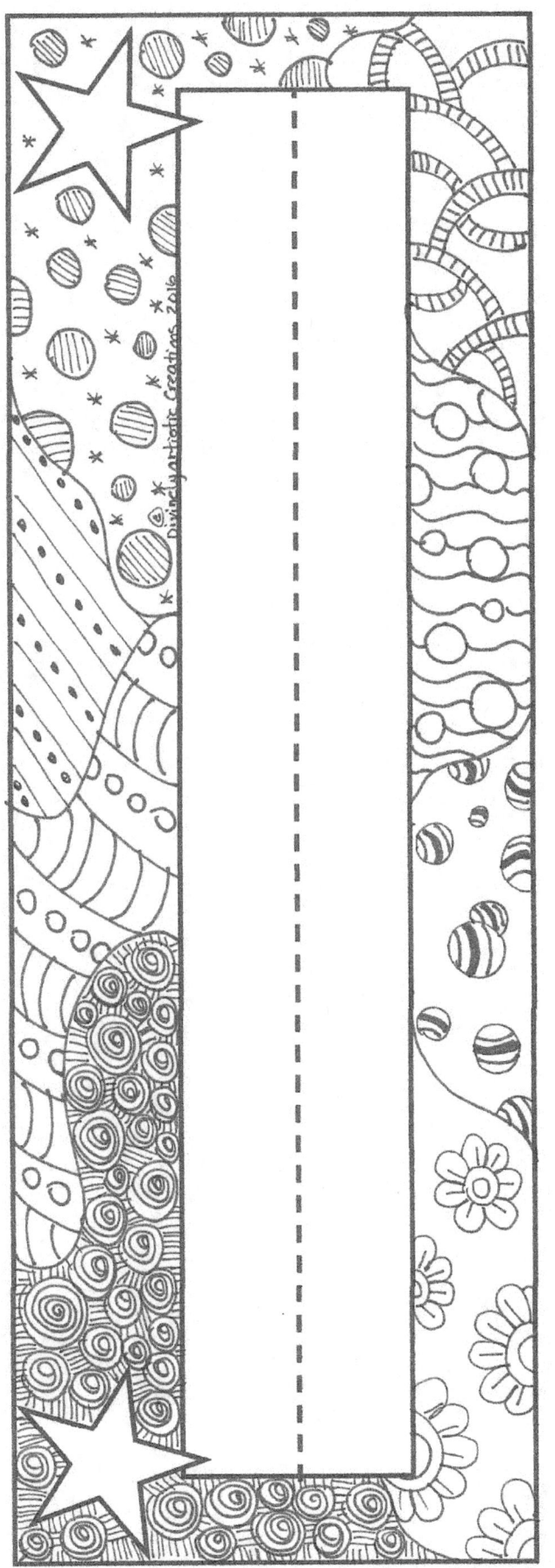
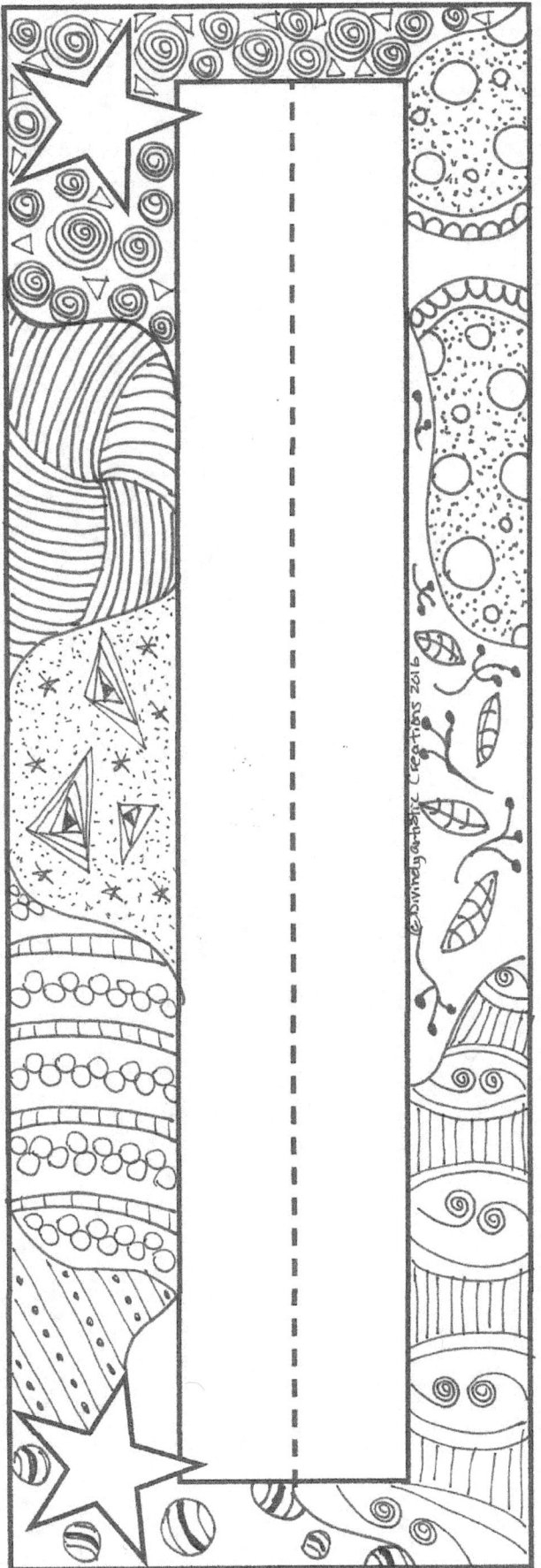

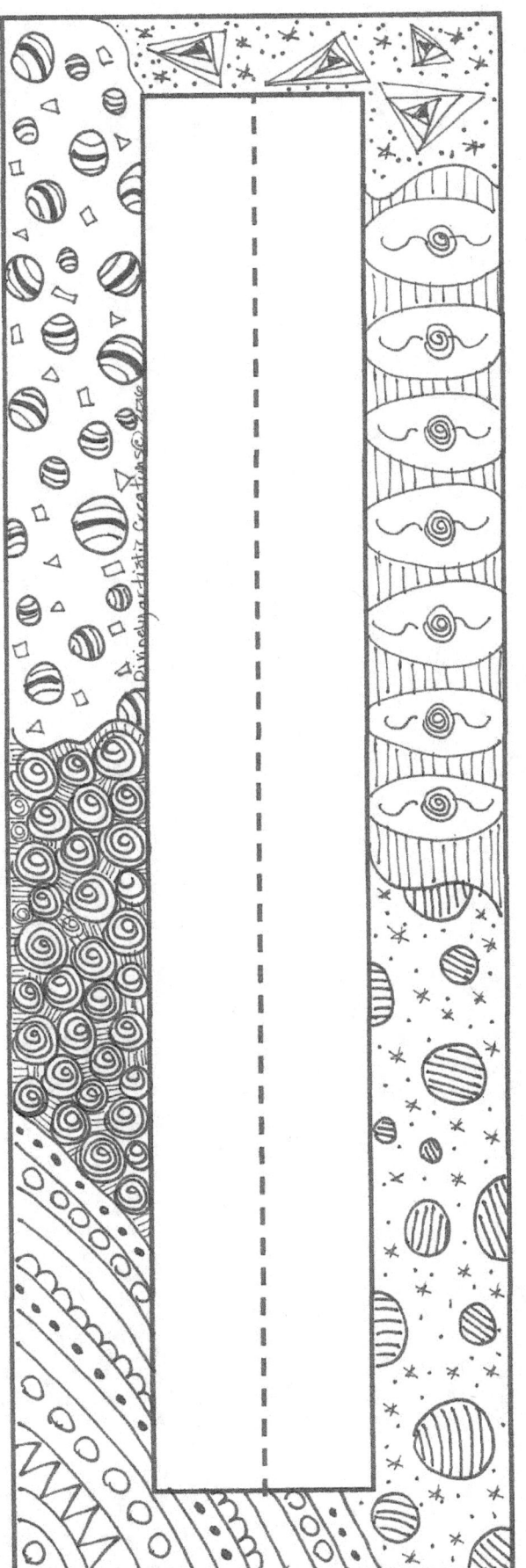

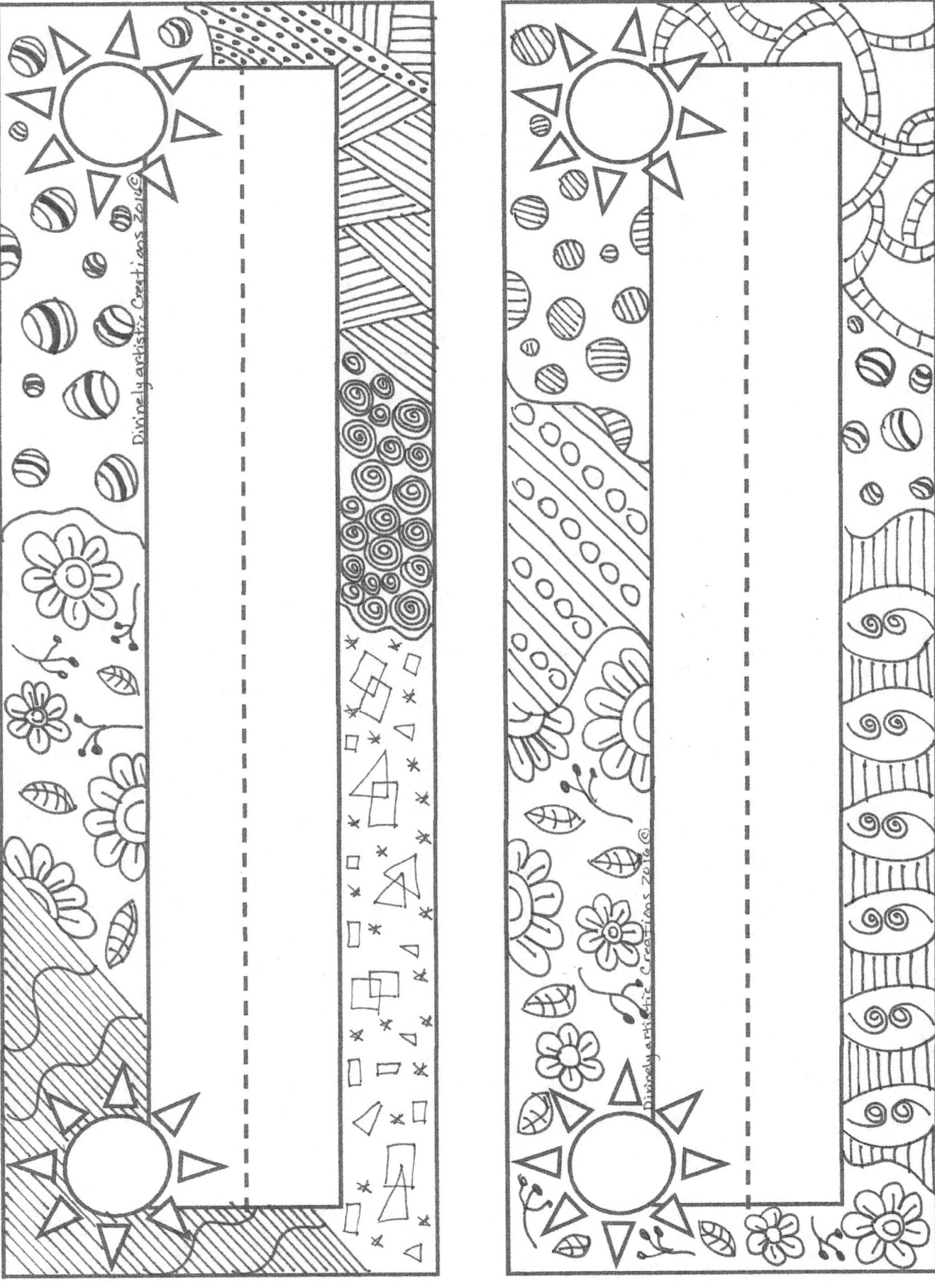

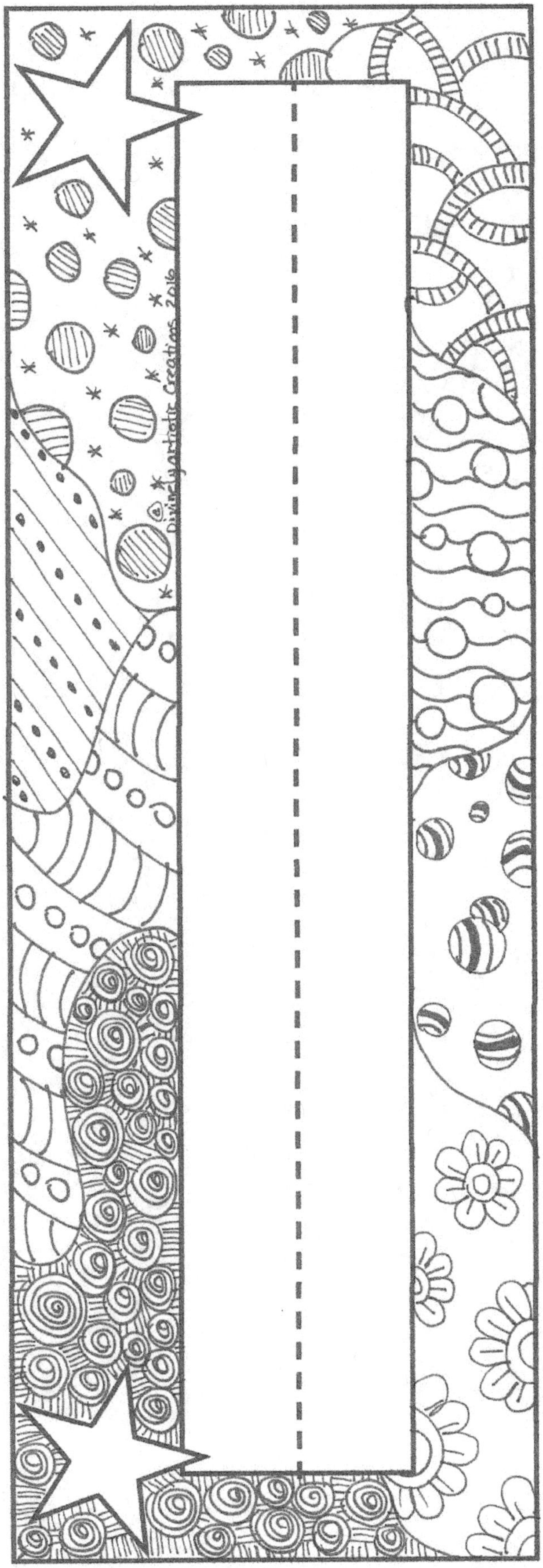

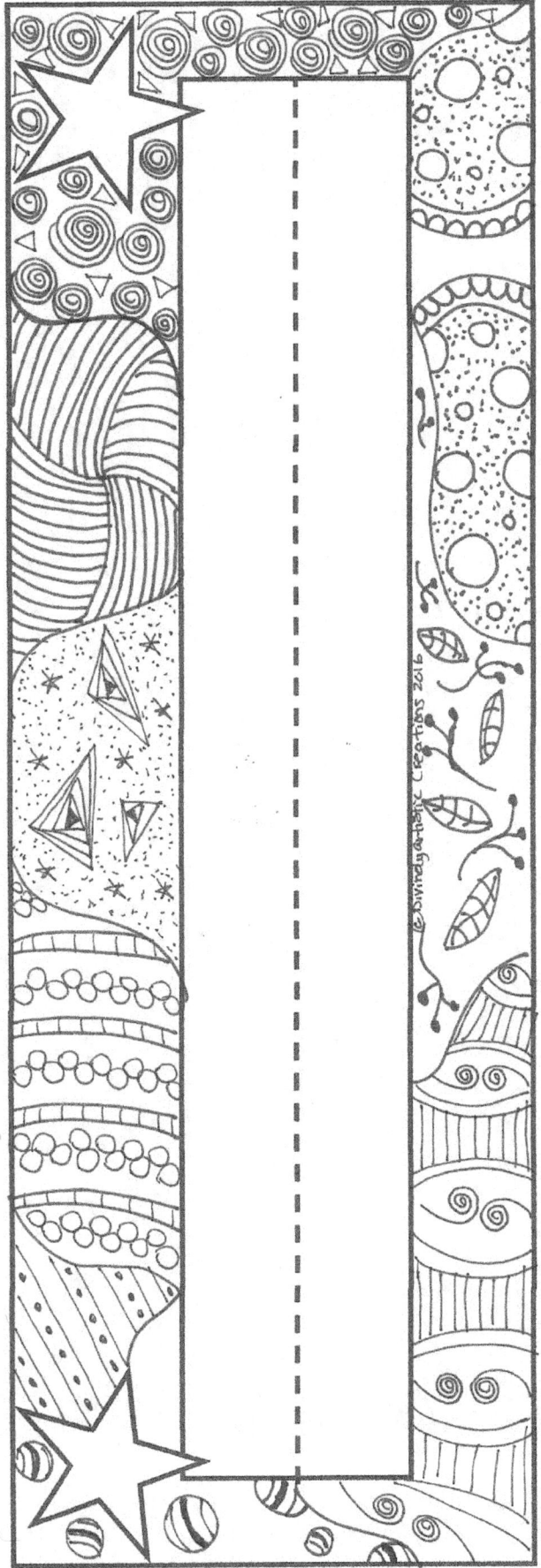

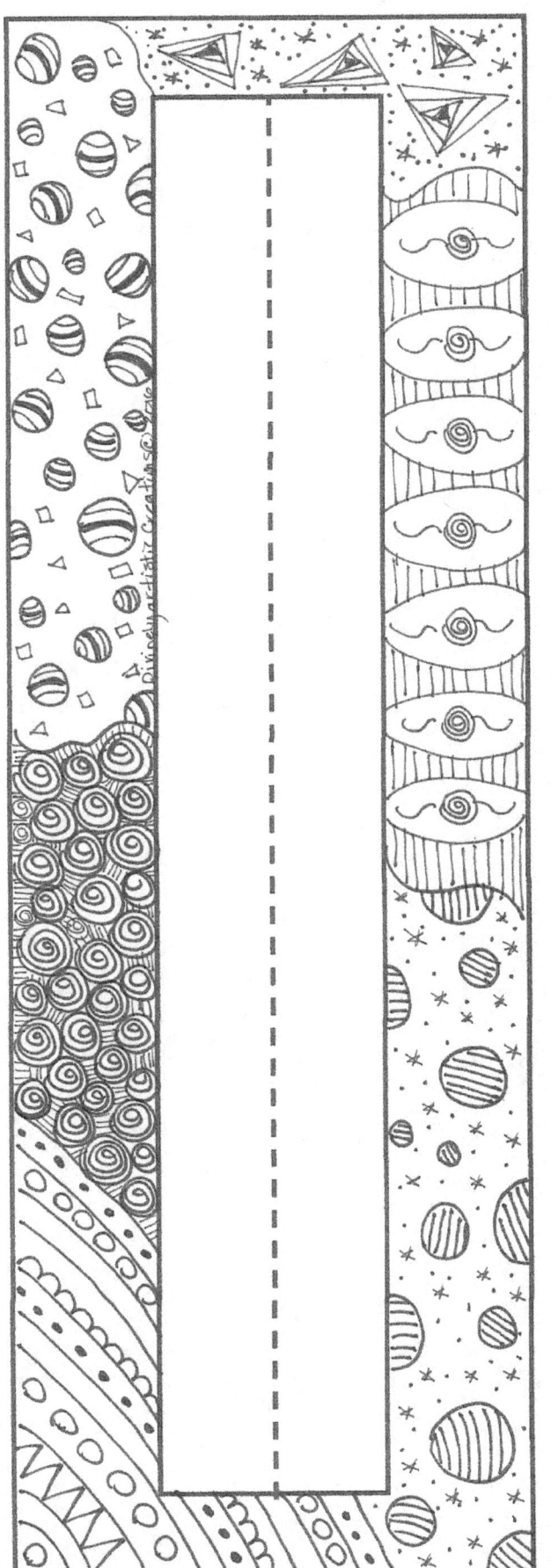

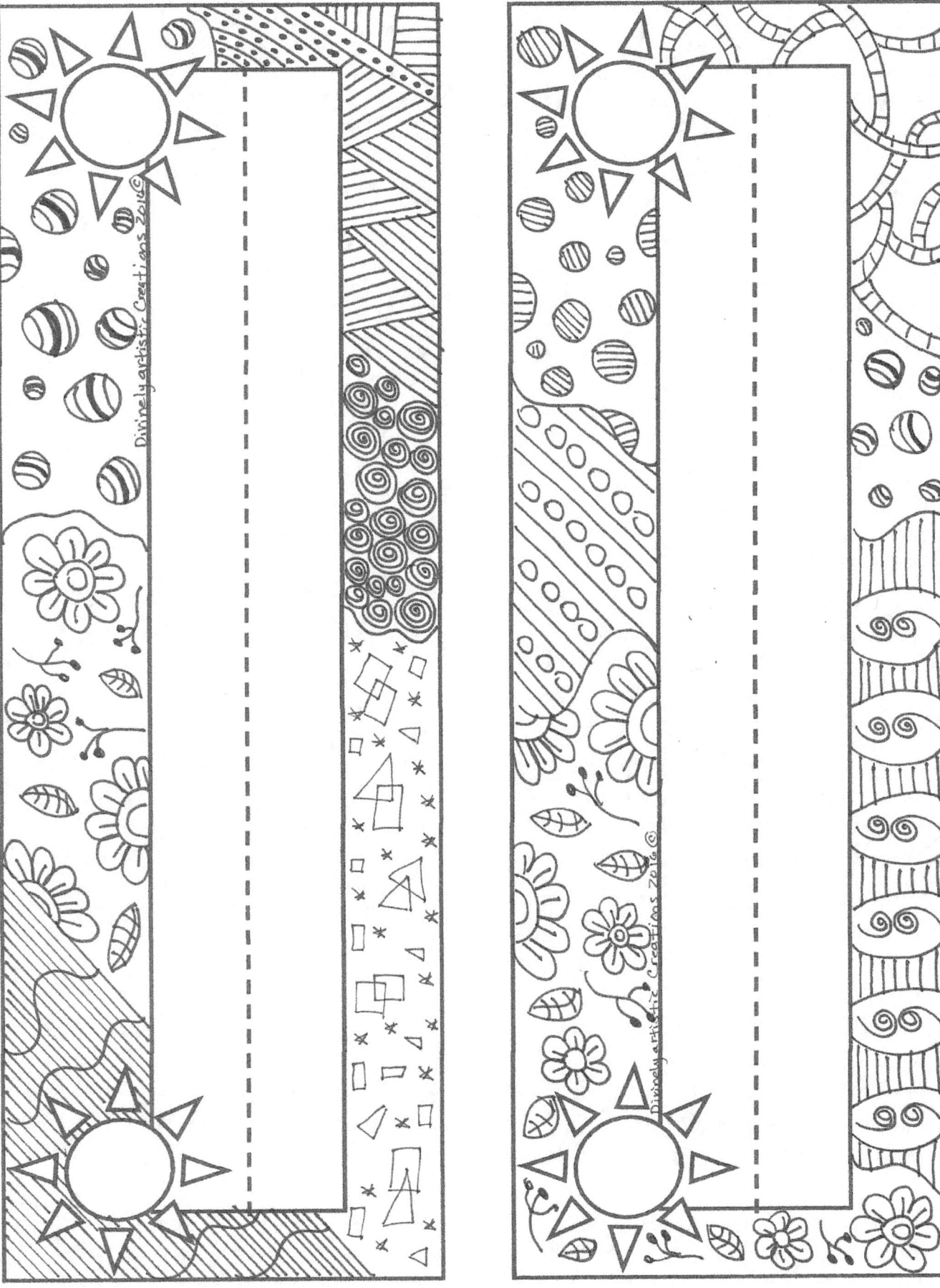

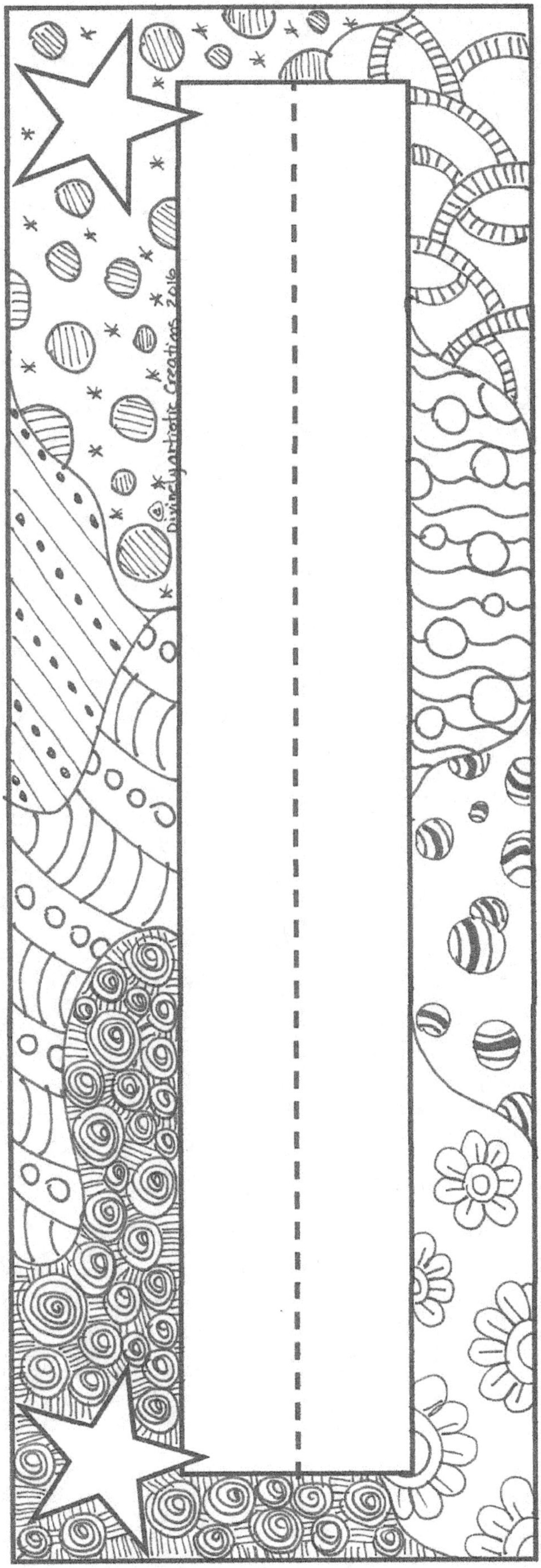

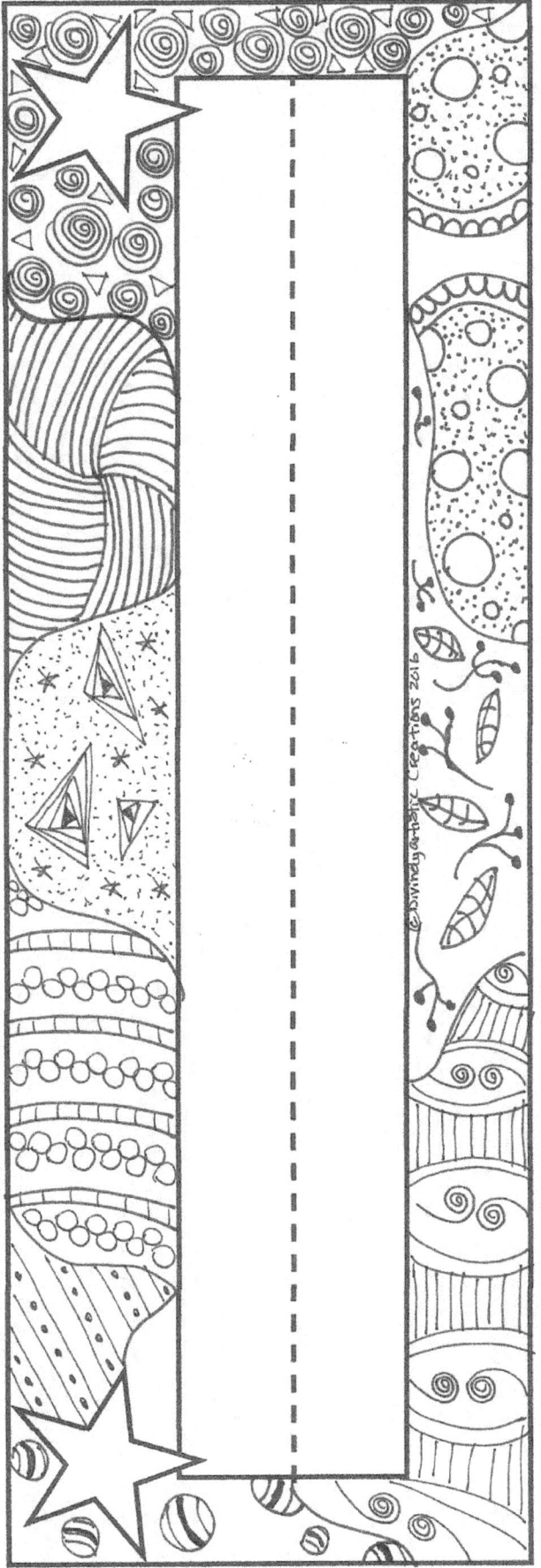

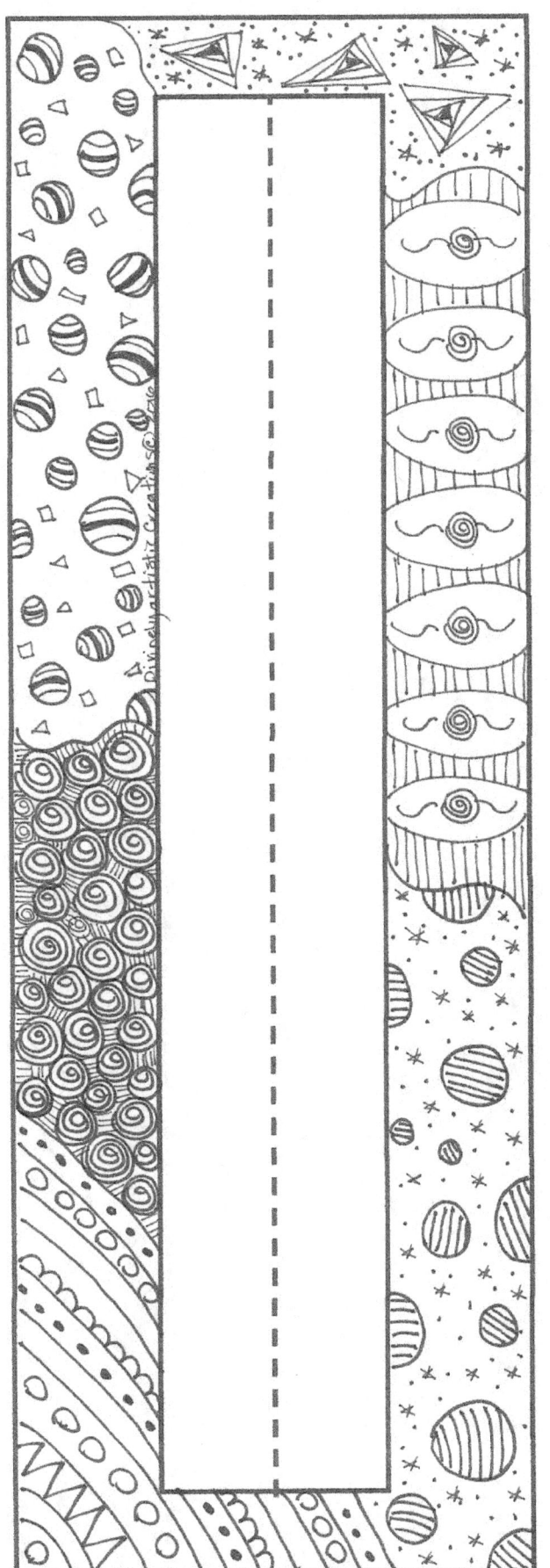
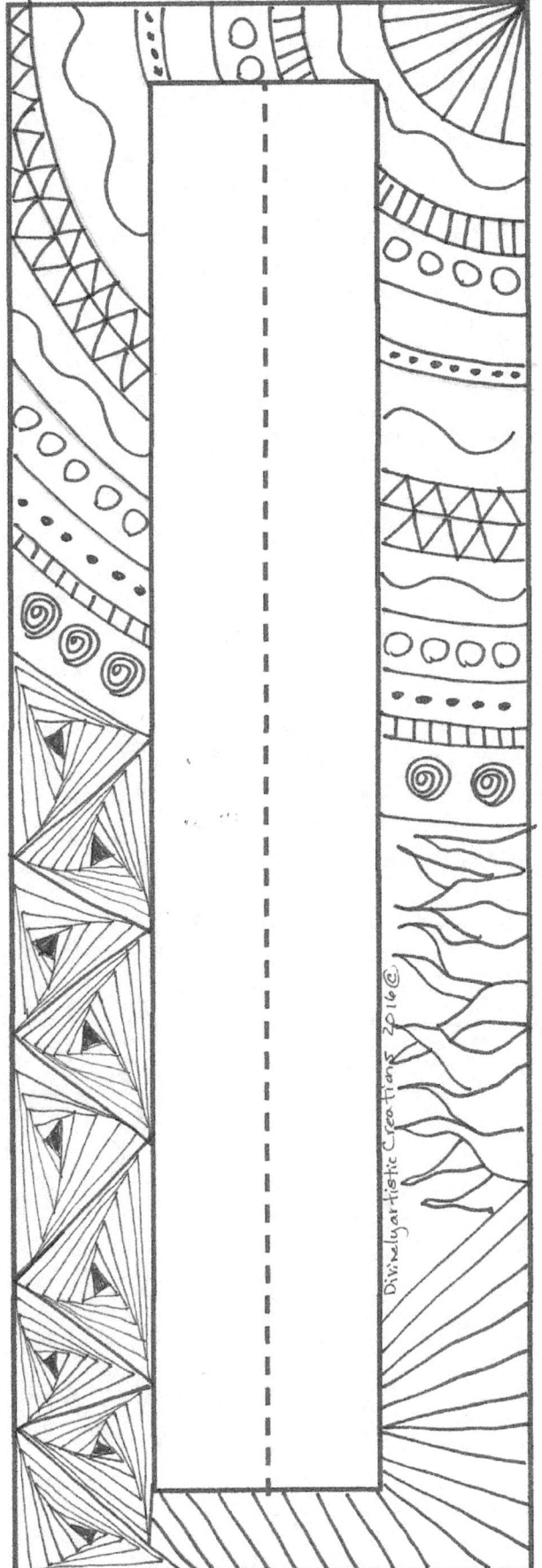

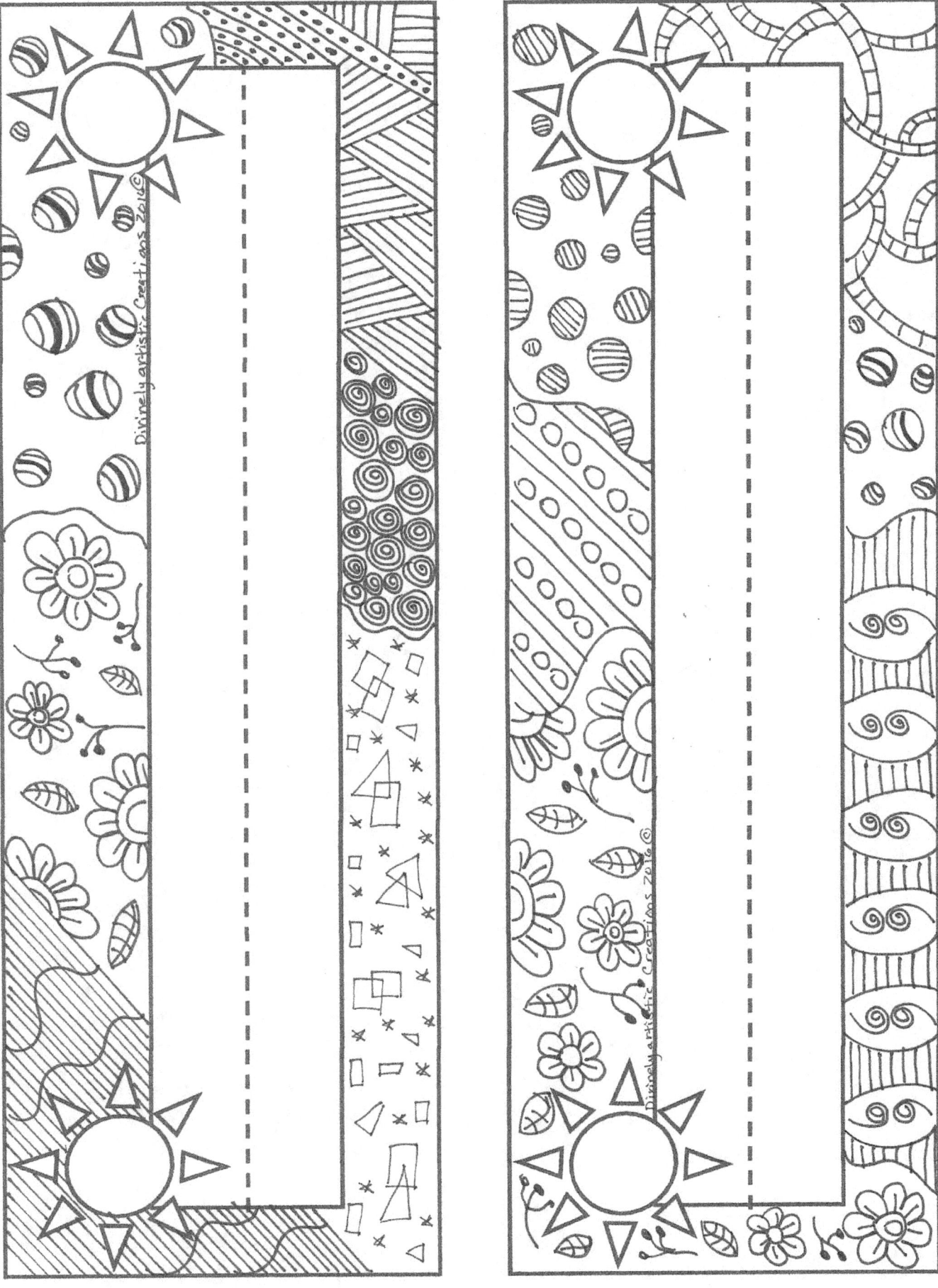

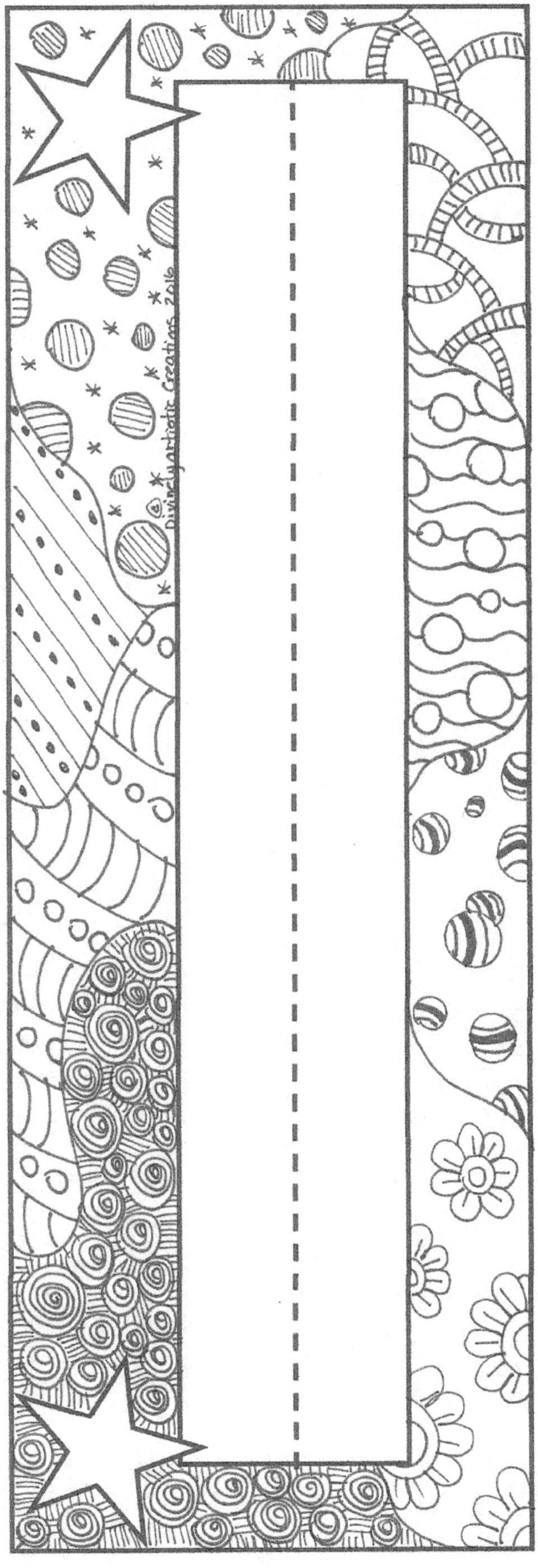

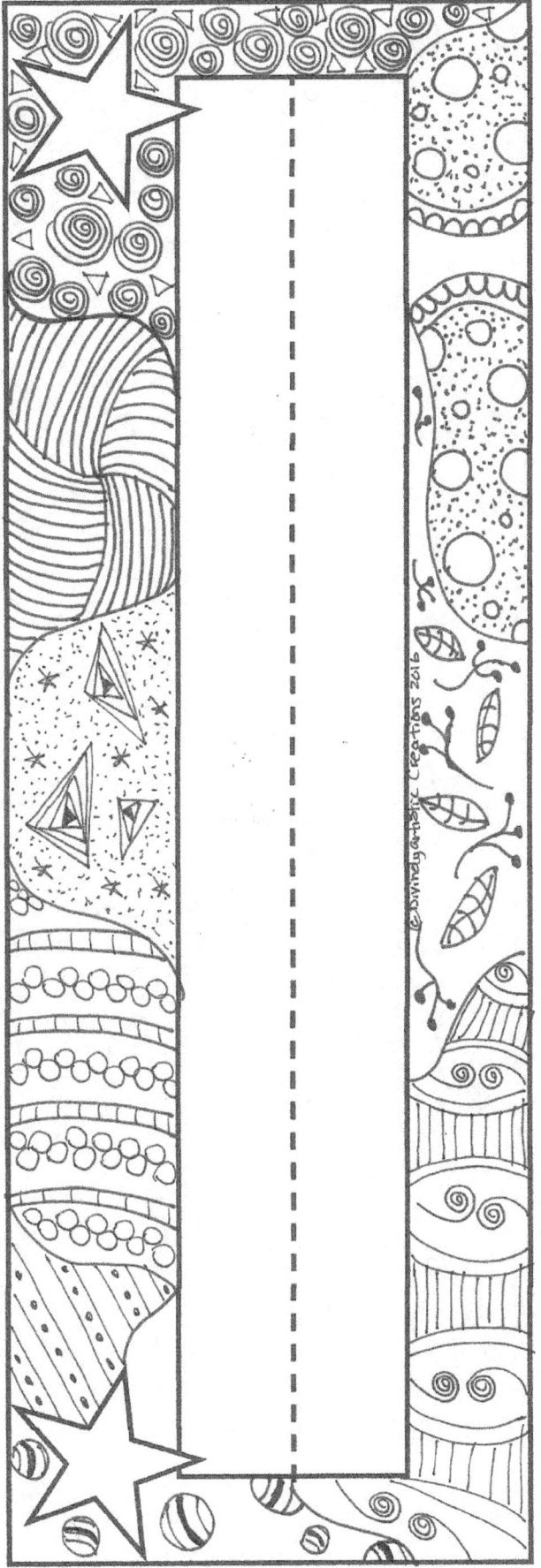

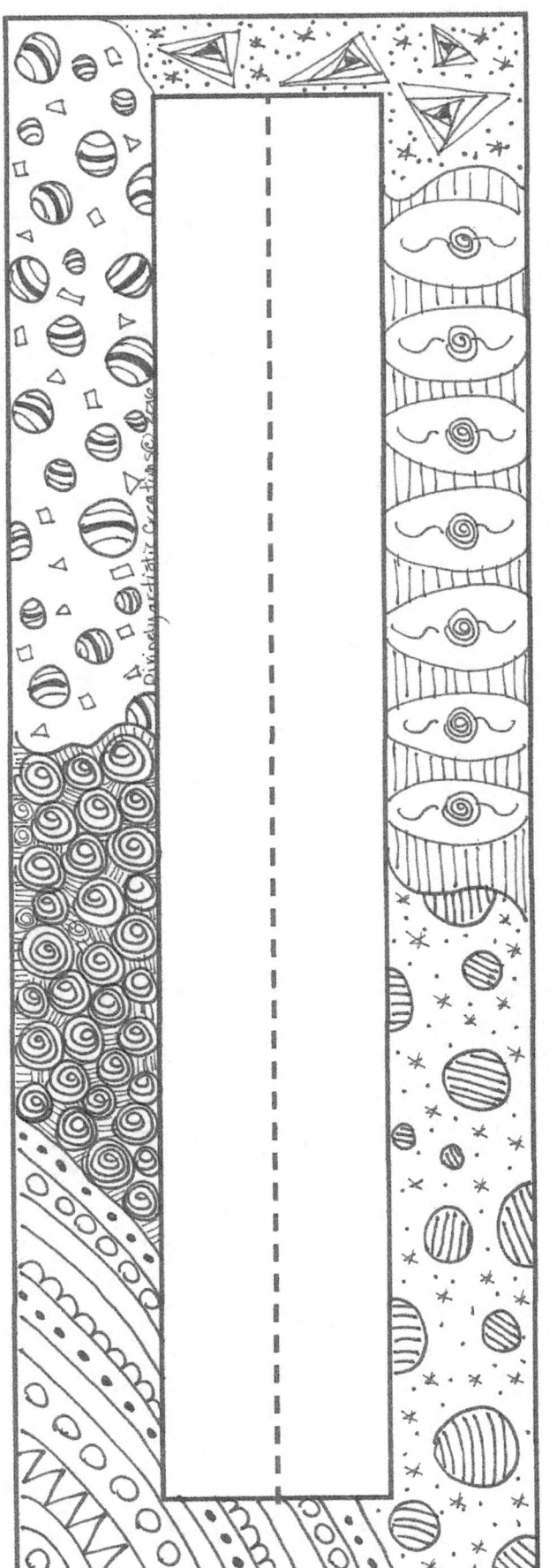

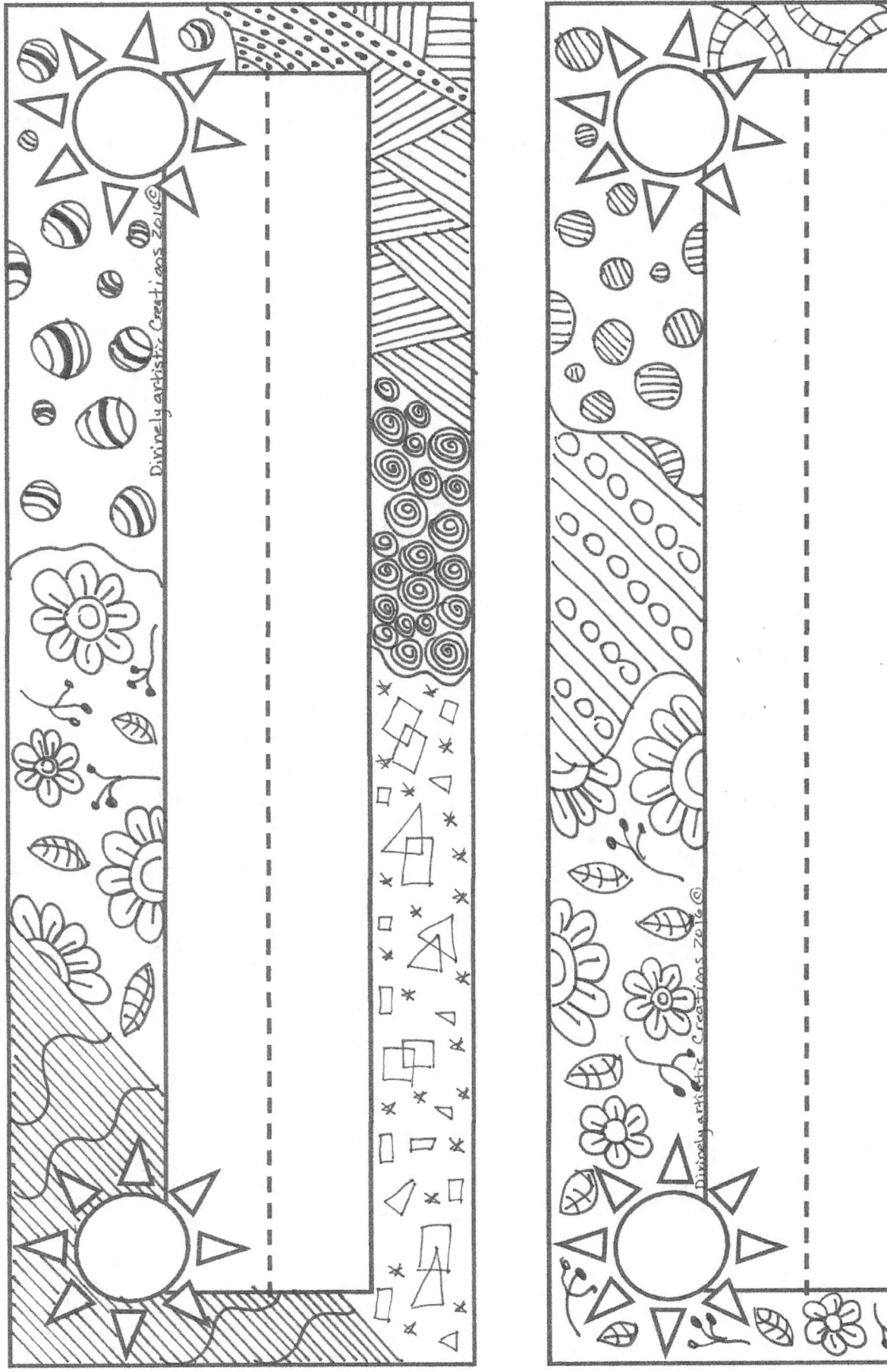

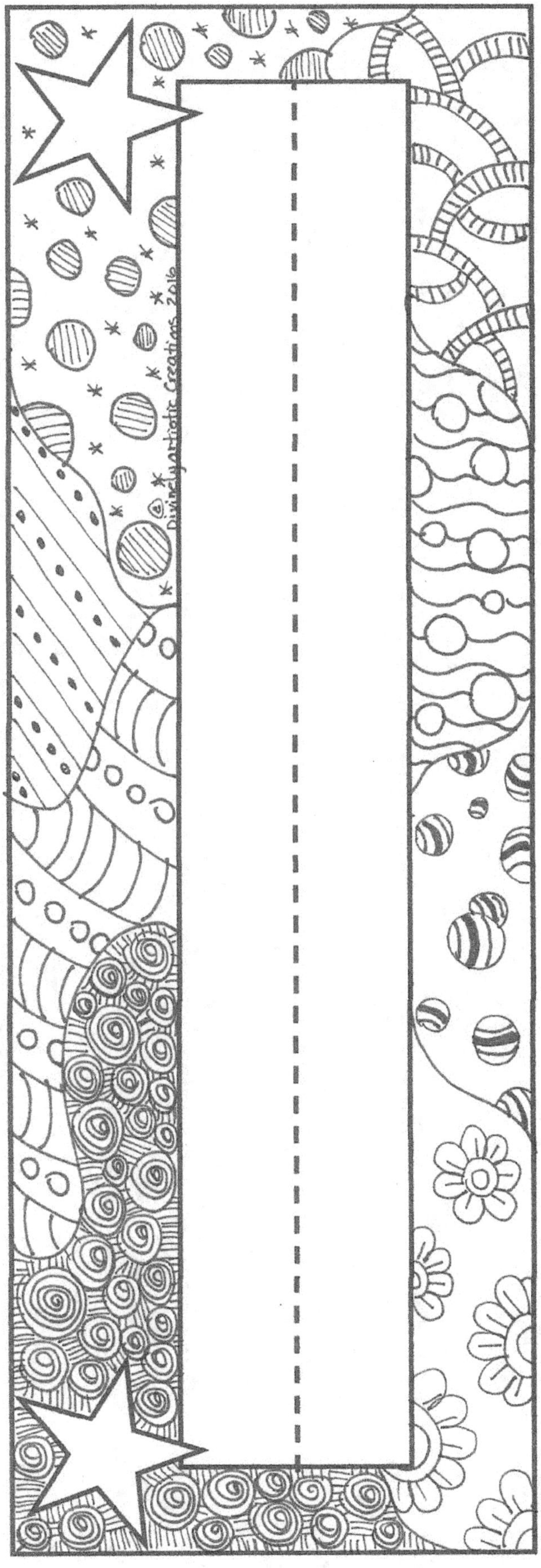

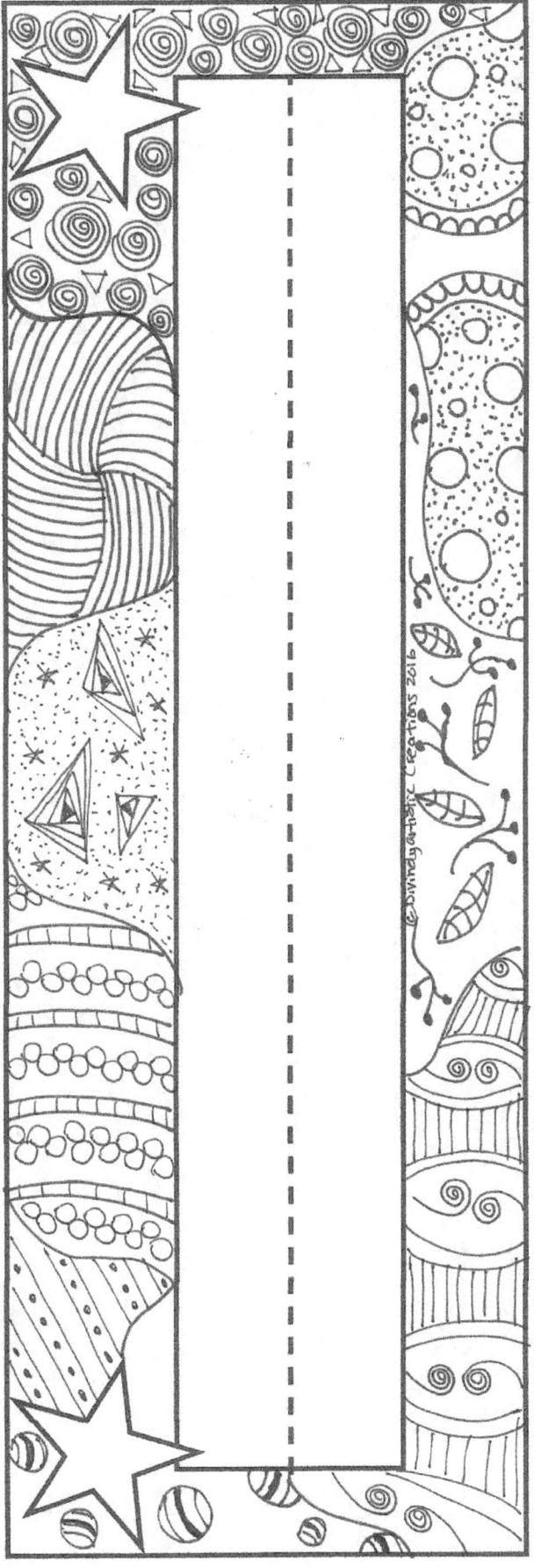